Primary Sources in U.S. History

Expansive America: 1877–1898

Jeanne M. Kish

Project Director
James A. Benedict

The Center for Learning

Jeanne M. Kish, a Martha Holden Jennings scholar and an experienced high school social studies teacher, earned her M.A. in history at Cleveland State University in Ohio. She wrote the following Center for Learning publications: *Antebellum America and Civil War: 1840–1865*, *America in Upheaval: The 1960s*, and *Grade 8 U.S. History*, Books 1 and 2. She served as Series Revision Editor for the Center's Basic Skills Series.

The Publishing Team

Rose Schaffer, M.A., President/Chief Executive Officer
Bernadette Vetter, M.A., Vice President
Lora Murphy, M.A., Vice President, Social Studies Division
Tammy Sanderell, B.A., Editor

Cover Design

Susan Chowanetz Thornton, B.S.

List of credits found on Acknowledgments page beginning on 106.

ISBN 1-56077-679-X

Contents

Series Introduction

The *Primary Sources in U.S. History* series is designed to encourage a sense of connection to the past, an appreciation of different perspectives and cultures, and further investigation of the people who made history in the United States. Students take part in the analysis and interpretation of various types of documents, applying critical-thinking skills to discover more about the major political, social, and economic movements in American history. They become active investigators who must defend, alter, or abandon their positions when confronted with new information. They are challenged to make sense of history using the raw materials of the discipline.

These units complement those of The Center for Learning's four-unit senior high U.S. History series and its two Advanced Placement U.S. History units; all of which may be used creatively in conjunction with any textbook or course of study to enrich and deepen the study of American history.

The *Primary Sources in U.S. History* series is organized chronologically and thematically. Each of the fifteen units covers a major epoch in American history.

Colonization: 1521–1763

Revolution and Constitution: 1763–1791

Early Nation: 1791–1820

Jacksonian America: 1820–1840

Antebellum America and Civil War: 1840–1865

Reconstruction: 1865–1877

Expansive America: 1877–1898

America in the Age of Imperialism: 1898–1920

Interwar America: 1920–1940

America in World War II: The 1940s

Consensus and Conformity: The 1950s

America in Upheaval: The 1960s

Disillusioned America: The 1970s

America's Turn to the Right: The 1980s

Technological Revolution: The 1990s

Each unit contains one lesson on each of the following topics:

- Business and Labor
- Culture
- Everyday Life
- Immigration
- Larger World/Diplomacy
- Law and Society
- Minority Experience
- Politics
- Religion
- Women

Goals and Assumptions

1. History is an evolutionary process. To appreciate the present and look to the future, students need to examine that process and investigate how and why changes occur.
2. History is comprised of recurring themes. To understand the place these themes have in the present, students must analyze them and draw conclusions about them.
3. Understanding American society requires students to recognize the interrelationship of political, social, and cultural issues.
4. Students need certain skills (reading, writing, questioning, speaking, and thinking), so instruction and practice in these areas must be provided.

Objectives

1. To provide students with a knowledge base in American history
2. To enable students to read and digest factual information independently, in small groups, and in large group settings, in order to employ higher-level thinking skills
3. To develop the necessary skills in students that enable them to think clearly and communicate their ideas to others
4. To make students aware of commonalities and differences in the American community that have developed over time
5. To guide students in analyzing and assessing the point of view of historical actors
6. To help students understand and think critically about crucial issues and people in American history
7. To give students more experience with questioning sources, evaluating competing interpretations of facts, comparing and contrasting perspectives, understanding causation, and making reasonable arguments based upon evidence

Themes

1. Humans shape their behavior in response to universal human needs and values.
2. Conflict unresolved by compromise and change may lead to violence.
3. Cultures are constantly undergoing change.
4. Human behavior reflects adaptation to and modification of physical and human environments.
5. Individuals tend to interpret the past, present, and future in terms of their own values and points of view.
6. Specialization increases interdependence.
7. A democratic society encourages but does not insure equality.
8. Power can be used to achieve both constructive and destructive ends.
9. Through government and other institutions, humans modify and regulate their organizations to achieve goals of justice, stability, freedom, and growth.
10. Change is constant.

Concepts

1. Conflict
2. Commitment
3. Frame of reference
4. Opportunity
5. Freedom
6. Family
7. Causation
8. Evolution
9. Revolution
10. Historical interpretation
11. Equality
12. Government
13. Rights
14. Stability
15. Justice
16. Democracy
17. Participation
18. Nationalism
19. Dependence
20. Independence
21. Interdependence
22. Specialization
23. Behavior
24. Sectionalism
25. Work ethic
26. Leadership
27. Change
28. Reform
29. Culture
30. Industrialism
31. Urbanization
32. Cooperation
33. Environment
34. Decision making
35. Values
36. Expectations
37. Market economy
38. Wants and needs
39. Resources
40. Communication

Skills

1. Interpret what is read by drawing inferences.
2. Detect cause-and-effect relationships.
3. Assume the perspective of the other person.
4. Decode maps.
5. Read for a variety of purposes.
6. Interpret various forms of printed and visual materials.
7. Draw logical conclusions.
8. Evaluate sources of information.
9. Prepare summaries, position papers, and other written materials.
10. Identify bias in printed and visual materials.
11. Group data in categories according to appropriate criteria.
12. State relationships between categories of information.
13. Recognize the values implicit in issues and the possible courses of action that flow around them.
14. Predict likely outcomes based on factual information.
15. Identify instances in which more than one interpretation of factual materials is valid.
16. Extract significant ideas from supporting, illustrative details.
17. Restate major ideas of a complex topic in concise form.
18. Form opinions based on critical examination of relevant information.
19. Communicate effectively both orally and in writing.
20. Listen carefully for information.

Using Series Materials

In the *Primary Sources in U.S. History* series, students use many types of documents, including newspapers; letters; diaries; manuscripts; published tracts of political, social, or cultural significance; government documents; artwork; photographs; advertisements; and documents of everyday life, such as personal bills, report cards, and cookbooks. Activities for each lesson incorporate one or more of these sources to give students the flavor of the era and to encourage independent, collaborative, and creative thinking, problem solving, and decision-making. Separate lessons from any unit in the series may supplement textbook readings on a selected topic. Lessons on a particular theme may be used in current issues courses as background material or integrated into various topical electives in history. Teachers may prefer to borrow the procedures of a lesson while substituting a document of their own choosing. Or, conversely, teachers may want to reproduce only the document and experiment with a different approach to teaching the lesson.

While this series focuses on the historical content or importance of primary sources, lessons do not guide students through a step-by-step examination of the source itself. The appendix of each unit contains primary source analysis worksheets from the Education Branch of the National Archives. Throughout the lessons, procedures recommend that the appropriate worksheet be reproduced and distributed to accompany the lesson. Using the worksheet will guide students through a brief examination of the source itself. The forms are not complicated or lengthy, and clearly set the stage for students to assume the role of historian. To this end, a sample lesson using an analysis form from the appendix is presented at the beginning of each unit in the series. The sample lesson should be examined carefully and then used to familiarize students with using primary sources.

Each lesson in the series contains at least one student handout as well as a primary source. The handouts provide either in-class activities or homework activities. Although most handouts are intended for distribution to students, some may be used effectively as transparencies. In the handouts, the original spelling of the primary source has been maintained. To avoid distracting the reader, most of these are not marked [sic]. The lessons are intended to suggest meaningful class activities, but are in no way intended to substitute for textbook reading. Each lesson should always be correlated to the appropriate section of the class textbook. Finally, it is essential that the teacher read the lessons in advance to note appropriate assignments, to prepare needed materials for distribution, and to tailor the instruction to a particular class.

Unit Introduction

This unit in the *Primary Sources in U.S. History* series provides ten lessons about history during America's Age of Expansion. Each lesson is constructed around one or more primary sources of historical importance. The intent of each lesson is for students to learn more about a specific topic of an era by studying a piece of actual history, instead of reading the conclusions reached by a historian. In this process of learning history from primary sources, students use a variety of materials and approaches that promote critical thinking, reading, and writing, as well as other skills in mastering the concepts of the lessons.

The ten lessons in this unit deal directly with some of the important topics during America's period of expansion, both as a country and a world power, between 1877 and 1898. Topics such as the violence of the Homestead Steel Strike, the attempts to exclude Chinese immigration, the establishment of the Salvation Army to serve the poor of America's large urban centers, the role of women in the workforce of the west, and the annexation of Hawaii are included. One lesson deals with P. T. Barnum and the circus and examines the beginnings of the type of promotional activities so familiar to us today. Another lesson deals with the different interpretations of events in the west and examines excerpts from a soldier's journal and drawing made by a Native American, who used visual images to recount the Battle of the Little Big Horn. Other lessons deal with the capture of the outlaw, John Wesley Hardin, by the Texas Rangers, the experience of African-American soldiers in the Spanish-American War, and the assassination of President James A. Garfield.

Each lesson contains all needed teacher and student materials. Read the lessons in advance to note appropriate assignments and prepare the necessary materials for distribution to the class. Advance preparation also provides the opportunity for you to modify the lesson to suit your goals and tailor it to the needs of your class.

Review the sample lesson and handout. Using the sample lesson to introduce primary sources to student is strongly recommended. The appropriate analysis form should be used to aid the analysis of every primary source in the unit. At the very least, the forms should be used the first few times that students work with primary source material. This will encourage them to question the sources with which they are working. Finally, always correlate the lesson and handouts to the appropriate sections of your basal classroom textbook.

Answers will vary unless otherwise indicated. Students may need additional paper to complete some handouts.

Cross-Reference Chart

This cross-reference chart provides an evaluation of the unit's lessons based on the concepts, themes, and skills outlined as integral to the *Primary Sources in U.S. History* series (see Series Introduction). The chart offers an analysis of the incorporation of major themes and concepts and details each lesson's development of specific critical-thinking skills.

Lesson	Concepts	Themes	Skills
1	1, 2, 7, 15, 30, 34, 37	2, 8	5, 6, 8, 17, 19
2	10, 29	5	6, 19
3	1, 3, 10, 29, 40	4, 5	1, 6, 8, 15
4	1, 4, 5, 11, 15, 16	1, 3, 5, 7	1, 6, 8, 10, 16
5	1, 7, 9, 10, 13, 16, 18, 34, 39	2, 3, 5, 8	1, 2, 5, 7, 13, 17
6	1, 13, 15, 23, 34	5, 8, 9	1, 5, 8, 18, 19
7	1, 2, 11, 17, 25, 26, 32, 35, 36	1, 3, 4, 7	1, 5, 6, 8, 17, 19
8	1, 9, 12, 15, 16, 23, 34	2, 8	1, 5, 6, 8, 17, 19
9	2, 17, 21, 22, 26, 27, 28, 32, 34, 35	1, 9	1, 5, 6, 8
10	3, 4, 5, 11, 17, 22, 23, 25, 27	3, 4, 10	1, 6, 8, 16, 19

Sample Lesson

Getting Back What's Mine

Objective

- To become familiar with a primary source through completion of a primary source analysis worksheet

Notes to the Teacher

This lesson's primary source document is an "Application for Effects of a Deceased Member" from about 1910. The document shows that H. W. Tappe is going to apply for the effects of his father, August Tappe, who died August 5, 1910.

Analysis of the form's first page shows that August Tappe had been a member of the 17th West Virginia Infantry (Civil War) and was residing at the Central Branch of the National Home for Disabled Volunteer Soldiers at the time of his death. From this it can be presumed that he was disabled. One can also presume that his wife preceded him in death, since a section of the form to be used for a claim by a widow is crossed out and his son is applying. The form shows that there were at least five children other than H. W. Tappe, four of whom are named—note the blanks for signatures at the bottom. Someone has written on the form for H. W. Tappe the signatures he will need (all children of August Tappe and the children of any deceased children of August Tappe) and not need (his own). The form also states on the side that the signatures must be witnessed by two persons. This was probably a practice form since it did not have all of the signatures, hadn't been witnessed, and wasn't turned in. Page two of the form, while not strictly necessary for the exercise, is provided. Much interesting history can be gained from reading the formal document a son needed to file to receive the effects of his deceased father.

The form was found in a box in the attic of one of the authors of this series. August Tappe was his great-grandfather and Henry Wadsworth Tappe was his grandfather. Henry was one of thirteen children, seven of whom were no longer living by 1910. Four died before the age of one, one died at age five, and one died at age seven. The seventh, William, died at age 25 of yellow fever in the Philippines shortly after the Spanish-American War. The missing name by the 5 in the blanks for signatures was Louis Tappe; it is not known if he ever signed. Typical of studying historical documents, the question of whether or not Henry ever obtained his father's effects is still unanswered.

Procedure

1. Begin by asking students if they know what a *primary source* in history is. After students have suggested definitions, ask them what they think of this definition:

   primary source—source created by people who actually saw or participated in an event and recorded that event or their reactions to it immediately after the event

   Point out that this definition ignores the type of source and focuses on what makes it primary. To complete the sample lesson in one class period, limit the discussion to five minutes.
2. Distribute **Handouts 26** and **A** for students to study and complete. Monitor and assist as necessary.
3. Toward the end of class, share and discuss students' answers, especially 6a and 6e. Ask students what else can be learned from the form. Refer to Notes to the Teacher.
4. Debrief by distributing **Handout B.** Help students compare the form they completed with **Handout B**.
5. Distribute another copy of **Handout 26.** Assign students to find a document from their family history and to complete a written source analysis for that document. Encourage students to involve their parents and others in this assignment.
6. Conclude by asking volunteers to share their documents and completed forms.

Extension Activity

After sharing Notes to the Teacher information, ask students to theorize how six of thirteen children died as children. Some brief research may be necessary. (*Responses could include medical care in the era, the value of having children in spite of the high incidence of childhood deaths, poverty and/or the role of women in such a society.*) Have students list the signatures Henry Tappe needed to have his father's effects returned.

Name ______________________

Date ______________________

Getting Back What's Mine

Read the following document and complete the appropriate document analysis form.

[38—a]

APPLICATION FOR EFFECTS OF DECEASED MEMBER

(TO BE USED IN ALL CASES.)

TO THE GOVERNOR,

Central Branch,

National Home for Disabled Volunteer Soldiers.

SIR:

I hereby make application for the effects of August Tappe, deceased, late C Co., 17" Regiment W. Va. Inf, who died at CENTRAL BRANCH, N.H.D.V.S on 5" August 1910 as his Son

~~H. W. Tappe [illegible]~~

Address 647 Euclid Ave. Cleveland O

(TO BE USED IN CASE OF CLAIM BY WIDOW.)

STATE OF .... }
COUNTY OF .... } ss.

We, the undersigned, hereby certify that the above named .... is the identical person she represents herself to be, and is known as the widow of .... deceased.

Subscribed and sworn to before me, this .... day of ...., 191....

(TO BE USED IN THE CASE OF TWO OR MORE HEIRS.)

We the undersigned, heirs of August Tappe, deceased, hereby authorize H. W. Tappe to receive and receipt for all of his effects in the possession of the National Home for Disabled Volunteer Soldiers.

All other Children, except H.W. and Children of deceased Children if any Sign here.

1 A. C. Tappe
2 Jennie Eschelbach
3 Mathilde B. Lehman
4 Edward Tappe
5

Signatures by mark must have 2 witnesses

Name ____________________

Date ____________________

Cleveland Ohio
Republic Building
647. Euclid Ave
.............................., 191......

H. W. Tappe
Son

APPLICATION FOR EFFECTS

OF

August Tappe

Late ..C.. Co., ..17th.. Reg't. ..W. Va Inf

WHO DIED AT

..Central.. Branch, N. H. for D. V. S.,

..5th August.., 191..0

(Form 38—a.)

(6—15—'06.)

.... Branch, N. H. for D. V. S.,

.............................., 191......

Respectfully forwarded to..............................

....

Manager National Home for D. V. S., for such action as he deems proper.

....
Governor.

....

....

Respectfully returned to..............................

.... Governor

.... Branch, N. H. for D. V. S.,

....

....

....

....
Manager N. H. for D. V. S.

.... Branch, N. H. for D. V. S.,

.............................., 191......

Respectfully referred to the Quartermaster and to the Treasurer.

The Board of Managers having through..............................

.... approved this application the effects will be turned over, taking proper vouchers. The application to be filed in the Treasurer's office.

By order of the Governor.

....
Adjutant.

The order of the Board of Managers in this case has been obeyed.

.... Quartermaster.

.... Treasurer.

Name ______________________

Date ______________________

Written Document Analysis Worksheet*

1. Type of document (check one):

____ Newspaper	____ Map	____ Advertisement
____ Letter	____ Telegram	____ Congressional record
____ Patent	____ Press release	____ Census report
____ Memorandum	____ Report	X Other *request for deceased family member's effects*

2. Unique physical qualities of the document (check one or more):

____ Interesting letterhead	____ Seals	____ Other ______
____ Handwritten	X Notations	
____ Typed	____ "Received" stamp	

3. Date(s) of document: *death occurred August 5, 1910*

4. Author (or creator) of the document: *National Home for Disabled Volunteer Soldiers and H. W. Tappe*

   Position (title): ______________________

5. For what audience was the document written? *addressed to the "Governor" Central branch of the NHDVS*

6. Document information (There are many possible ways to answer a-e.)

   a. List three things the author said that you think are important.

      1. *Tappe had to apply for his father's effects.*

      2. *The father served in 17th West Virginian Infantry.*

      3. *All living children had to apply.*

   b. Why do you think this document was written?

      to get his father's effects

   c. What evidence in the document helps you to know why it was written? Quote from the document.

      title of form—application for effects of deceased member

   d. List two things the document tells you about life in the United States at the time it was written:

      1. *numerous branches for homes for disabled veterans of the Civil War*

      2. *large family of six children*

   e. Write a question to the author that is left unanswered by the document:

      Did he file the form and obtain his father's effects?

*Adapted from worksheets developed by the staff of the Education Branch, National Archives, Washington, DC 20408.

Lesson 1—Business and Labor

The Homestead Steel Strike

Objectives

- To examine the causes and results of the Homestead Steel Strike of 1892
- To define business and industry's attitude toward unions in late nineteenth-century America

Notes to the Teacher

The relationship between business and labor in America during the late nineteenth century was characterized by violent strikes engineered by workers who often had anarchistic leanings and the virulent antiunion positions taken by owners and management. In 1892, a nation already reeling from instability brought on by economic depression, was confronted with a labor dispute at the Carnegie Mills of Homestead, Pennsylvania, which dominated the front pages of America's newspapers for over five months.

In this lesson, students examine and discuss documentary evidence regarding the circumstances leading up to the confrontation at the Homestead mill and create a three- to four-minute vignette portraying the position of either labor or management in the strike.

Reminder to Teachers

- Decide if the appropriate primary sources analysis worksheets from the appendix will be used in this lesson.
- Assign those sections of the basal textbook that are relevant to this lesson.

Procedure

1. Ask students if any members of their family have ever participated in a strike. Ask if any of those strikes involved violence on the part of management or labor. Ask for examples of why violence might break out (*people crossing the picket lines, the use of strike breakers, verbal confrontations between management representatives or labor*). Distribute **Handout 1.** Have students read it and be prepared for discussion. Conduct a class discussion of the Homestead Strike. Students should have a firm understanding of the conflict between labor and management in nineteenth-century America before proceeding to the next step.
2. Divide the class in half. Explain that one half of the class will represent labor, and the other management. Distribute **Handout 2** to those students representing labor and **Handout 3** to students representing management. Review students' responses.

Suggested Responses, Handout 2:

Part A.

1. *a fair wage, the right to economic independence, respectability, and the means to educate their children*
2. *If they united, the union could win; there was strength in numbers; together they could achieve what one person would not.*
3. *They would only demand a fair wage and take no undue advantage of their employers.*
4. *to reestablish a prosperous iron trade in America; to ensure job security for its workers; to improve the moral, physical, and intellectual condition of its workers; to blunt the hostility of management and resentment of the public towards unions*

Part B.

1. *not to dock and disembark from their barges, in order to avoid bloodshed*
2. *escort them through the mill, explain their position, not damage property*

Suggested Responses, Handout 3:

Part A.

1. *Carnegie was recognizing the fact that there were more nonunion (unskilled) workers than union (skilled) workers. The union was not representing the majority of the employees in the mills.*
2. *He believed that wages would not be affected because workers at two other mills owned by the corporation, which were nonunion, made higher wages than those at the Homestead plant.*
3. *Improvements would make it easier and more efficient for men to produce large amounts of high grade steel. Correspondingly, if they were paid by the amount*

of steel they produced, they would receive higher wages.

4. *the union agreement, which guaranteed the employment of a specific number of union members at the mill, even if they were not needed*
5. *Carnegie warned Frick that the men would not be happy with the proposal to become a nonunion plant and that he should be ready for trouble.*

Part B.

1. *supply three hundred men to provide protection for mill property and replacement employees*
2. *violent demonstrations; displaced workers and those who came to these events hoping to stir up trouble*
3. *The detective guards were not to be armed unless the occasion called for it. They were to protect property and workers.*
4. *It was to be conducted in secret.*
5. *They would be deputized.*

3. Distribute **Handout 4** and have students complete it. Review students' answers.

Suggested Responses:

Part A.

1. *There were about thirty or forty veterans of previous strikes, who were always employed by Pinkerton; most of the others had never participated in an action of this type.*
2. *of getting shot*
3. *The group leaders abandoned them.*
4. *The men on his boat spent most of the time huddled under tables and looking for protective cover. The strikers used sharpshooters to keep the Pinkertons under cover, a cannon to try to sink the barges, and sticks of dynamite to try to blow up the barges.*
5. *There was no tugboat to guide them, and the river directly below flowed into a falls.*

Part B.

1. *They were to be watchmen at the mill.*
2. *When they were about two miles from Homestead, whistles began to blow to warn of their arrival.*
3. *The first crowd tried to stop the barges from tying up and from putting out a plank to come ashore. The crowd tried to board the barges.*
4. *to take the wounded to Port Perry*
5. *Frick said that they would need arms if violence broke out.*

4. Divide students in each half of the class into groups of three or four. There should be an equal number of groups representing management and labor. Explain that each group is to use the information contained in the handouts to prepare a three- or four-minute vignette on the Homestead Strike. If representing management, students should stress the position of Andrew Carnegie—that he was within his rights to demand an end of the union, and that the steps he and Henry Clay Frick took were valid. If representing labor, students should explain their demands and rights to unionization. Have students make their presentations. Have students critique the presentation as to accuracy regarding the historical positions of both sides.

Extension Activities

1. Have students investigate and report on other famous strikes in U.S. History, such as the strikes in the mining fields of Colorado and the Molly Maguires.
2. Have students research and create a time line illustrating the development of fair labor practices in America during the nineteenth and twentieth centuries.

Name ____________________

Date ____________________

Labor v. Management: The Homestead Strike of 1892

Read the following selection, and be prepared for class discussion.

The relationship between business and labor in America during the late nineteenth century was characterized by violent strikes engineered by workers who often had anarchistic leanings, and the virulent antiunion positions taken by owners and management. In 1892, a nation, already reeling from instability brought on by economic depression, was confronted with a labor dispute which dominated the front pages of America's newspapers for over five months.

Founded in 1876, the Amalgamated Association of Iron and Steel Workers, which represented skilled mill workers in western Pennsylvania and the Ohio Valley, set as its goals the reestablishment of a prosperous iron trade, the protection of job security for its workers, and the improvement of the moral, intellectual, and social condition of its members. Union leaders hoped to promote a position of nonviolence, aimed at blunting the hostility of management and resentment of the public towards unionism. In 1887, the union aligned itself with the American Federation of Labor, and by 1892, membership had grown to over twenty thousand. Within the mills, pressures from skilled workers resulted in discrimination against "green hands." Societal pressures produced discriminatory practices against nonwhites. Mill employment and union membership were often limited to relatives of those already employed.

In July 1892, the Amalgamated Association of Iron and Steel Workers went on strike against the Carnegie Steel Corporation of Pittsburgh, founded by Andrew Carnegie. The town of Homestead, located seven miles east of Pittsburgh on the banks of the Monongahela River, was the site of the largest steel mill in the world. In 1889, the workers had struck the Homestead Mills, demanding and receiving a contract built around a sliding wage scale to be determined by the current market price of steel. The contract was to expire at the end of June 1892. Carnegie, fearing unfavorable public opinion if he opposed the workers' demands, scheduled a journey to Scotland and turned over control of Carnegie Steel to Henry Clay Frick.

Frick, notorious for his extreme antilabor sentiments, owned extensive coal fields in eastern Pennsylvania and supplied much of the coke used in Pittsburgh's iron and steel industry. Using tactics he had developed in coal field strikes, Frick assumed management of Carnegie Steel. Many believed Frick hated his employees. In his coal fields, unions were prohibited, employees were ruled with an iron hand, and the company always had the last word. In anticipation of a strike, Frick ordered the construction of a solid board fence topped with barbed wire surrounding the mill property, and turned the mills into a fortified camp, which was quickly dubbed "Fort Frick." Frick abolished the sliding scale and refused to negotiate with the union's representatives. As a form of protest, workers burned Frick and plant superintendent J. A. Potter in effigy. Sent to cut down the effigies, Frick's representatives were sprayed with water hoses by the steelworkers. On June 28, Frick ordered the mills shut down, stating that there was no strike, but rather a lockout. The striking workers organized along the lines of a military company and stationed guards at the entrances to the mill to prevent the entrance of scabs. Frick soon realized that his security force was inadequate to deal with the strikers and turned to the Pinkerton National Detective Agency for help. Both Carnegie and Frick had used Pinkertons during the late 1880s to protect strikebreakers. The Pinkertons had built their reputation by protecting the rights of business in the coal fields and steel mills of America, beginning in the 1850s with their infiltration and destruction of the "Molly Maguires," an organization of Irish miners who perpetrated extensive violence against coal companies in eastern Pennsylvania. Three hundred "special deputies" were to be brought by river barge up the Monongahela to the entrance of the Homestead Mills.

Name ______________________

Date ______________________

Early in the morning of July 6, workers who saw the approach of the barges sounded the alarm, and virtually the entire town converged on the riverbank. Once the workers realized the detectives planned to dock and enter the mill, they moved to stop them. Shots were fired, by whom is unknown, and the confrontation quickly deteriorated into a pitched battle. Workers laid down covering fire while the women and children in the crowd moved away from the gunfire. Hiding behind stacks of pig iron and scrap steel, the workers, using rifles and dynamite, battled the detectives for over thirteen hours. Finally, around 5 P.M., the Pinkerton detectives surrendered to the workers. Ten people died during the confrontation.

Governor Robert E. Pattison ordered the Pennsylvania National Guard to report to Pittsburgh and secure the mill. Within a week, the situation was under control. Frick then set out to punish the striking workers. He fired them all, hiring back a few who agreed to work under a nonunion contract agreement and blacklisting others. By mid-November, Homestead employees voted to return to work. Frick brought criminal charges against the leaders of the strike, charging them with inciting to riot and treason against the state of Pennsylvania. Arrested repeatedly, forced to post high bail, and ordered to provide restitution for damages to mill property, many workers lost what little money or property they had and were entangled in a series of court cases. Union organizers struggled for the next forty years to represent workers in Pittsburgh's mills.

Name ______________________

Date ______________________

The Union

Part A.

In 1890, 291 lodges of the Amalgamated Association of Iron and Steel Workers sent representatives to a twenty-two-day convention. The outcome of the convention reflected the concerns of the average mill worker, rather than the collective views of the union hierarchy. Read the following excerpt from the preamble to the Constitution of the Amalgamated Association of Iron and Steel Workers, and answer the questions.

AAISW Preamble, June 1892

Year after year the capital of the country becomes more and more concentrated in the hands of the few; and, in proportion, as the wealth of the country becomes centralized, its power increases and the laboring classes become more or less impoverished. It therefore becomes us as men who have to *battle* with the stern realities of life, to look this matter fair in the face. There is no *dodging* the question. Let every man give it fair, full, and candid consideration, and then act according to his honest convictions. What position are we, the Iron and Steel Workers of America, to hold in our society? Are we to receive an equivalent for our labor sufficient to maintain us in comparative independence and respectability, to procure the means with which to educate our children and qualify them to play their part in the world drama?

"In union there is strength," and in the formation of a National Amalgamated Association, embracing every Iron and Steel Worker in the country, a union founded upon a basis broad as the land in which we live lies our only hope. Single-handed we can accomplish nothing, but united there is no power of wrong we may not openly defy.

Let the Iron and Steel Workers of such places as have not already moved in this matter, organize as quickly as possible and connect themselves with the National Association. Do not be humbugged with the idea that this thing cannot succeed. We are not theorists; this is no visionary plan, but one eminently practicable. Nor can injustice be done to anyone; no undue advantage should be taken of any of our employers. There is not, there can not be any good reason why they should not pay us a fair price for our labor, and there is no good reason why we should not receive a fair equivalent therefor.

To rescue our trades from the condition into which they have fallen, and raise ourselves to that condition in society to which we, as mechanics, are justly entitled; to place ourselves on a foundation sufficiently strong to secure us from encroachments: to elevate the moral, social and intellectual condition of every Iron and Steel Worker in the country, is the object of our National Association.[1]

[1]Preamble to the Constitution of the Amalgamated Iron and Steel Workers, June 1892, in *The River Ran Red: Homestead 1892*, ed. David P. Demarest, Jr. (Pittsburgh: University of Pittsburgh Press, 1992).

Name ___________________________

Date ___________________________

1. What did the workers feel they were entitled to?

2. What did the members mean by "in union there is strength"?

3. What did the members promise their employers?

4. What were the aims of the union?

Part B.

Read the following excerpt dealing with the Homestead Steel Strike an answer the questions.

Hugh O'Donnell's Plea

> On behalf of five thousand men, I beg of you to leave here at once. I don't know who you are nor from whence you came, but I do know that you have no business here, and if you remain there will be more blood shed. We, the workers in these mills, are peaceably inclined. We have not damaged any property, and we do not intend to. If you will send a committee to us, we will take them through the works, carefully explain to them the details of this trouble, and promise them a safe return to their boats. But in the name of God and humanity, don't attempt to land! Don't attempt to enter these works by force.[2]

1. What did O'Donnell ask the Pinkertons to do and why?

2. What did O'Donnell promise the Pinkertons the strikers would do?

[2] U.S. House Report, 2447, 8, 133.

Name ____________________

Date ____________________

Management

Part A.

When a strike threatened the Carnegie Mills at Homestead, Pennsylvania, in 1892, Andrew Carnegie sent a notice to Henry Clay Frick, who managed the mills. Carnegie outlined his views on the use of the sliding scale and the reasoning behind his plan not to recognize the union as the bargaining agent of the workers when the labor contract expired in 1892. Frick failed to post the notices, and as a result, workers at the Homestead mill were unaware of Carnegie's position. The second selection outlines Carnegie's instructions to Frick regarding the labor situation at the mills. Read the documents dealing with the Homestead Steel Strike and answer the questions.

Notice to Employees at Homestead Works—April 4, 1892

These Works having been consolidated with the Edgar Thompson and Duquesne, and other mills, there has been forced upon this Firm the question Whether its Works are to be run 'Union' or 'Non-Union.' As the vast majority of our employees are Non-Union, the Firm has decided that the minority must give place to the majority. These Works therefore, will be necessarily Non-Union after the expiration of the present agreement.

This does not imply that the men will make lower wages. On the contrary, most of the men at Edgar Thomson and Duquesne Works, both Non-Union, have made and are making higher wages than those at Homestead, which has hitherto been Union.

The facilities and modes of working at Homestead Works differ so much from those of steel mills generally in Pittsburgh that a scale suitable for these is inapplicable to Homestead.

A scale will be arranged which will compare favorably with that at the other works named; that is to say, the Firm intends that the men at Homestead shall make as much as the men at either Duquesne or Edgar Thomson. Owing to the great changes and improvements made in the Converting Works, Beam Mills, Open Hearth Furnaces, etc., and the intended running of hot metal in the latter, the products of the works will be greatly increased, so that at the rates per ton paid at Braddock and Duquesne, the monthly earnings of the men may be greater than hitherto. While the number of men required will, of course, be reduced, the extensions at Duquesne and Edgar Thomson as well as at Homestead will, it is hoped, enable the firm to give profitable employment to such of its desirable employees as may temporarily be displaced. The firm will in all cases give the preferences to such satisfactory employees.

This action is not taken in any spirit of hostility to labor organizations, but every man will see that the firm cannot run Union and Non-Union. It must be either one or the other.[3]

Andrew Carnegie to Henry Clay Frick—June 10, 1892

As I understand matters at Homestead, it is not only the wages paid, but the number of men required by Amalgamated rules which makes our labor rates so much higher than those in the East.

Of course, you will be asked to confer, and I know you will decline all conferences, as you have taken your stand and have nothing more to say.

[3]"Notice to Empoyees at Homestead Works," 4 April 1892, in *The Inside History of the Carnegie Steel Company*, ed. James Howard Bridge (New York: Aldrine Book Company, 1903).

Name ______________________

Date ______________________

It is fortunate that only a part of the Works are concerned. Provided you have plenty of plates rolled, I suppose you can keep on with armor. Potter [the plant superintendent] will, no doubt, intimate to the men that refusal of scale means running only as Non-Union. This may cause acceptance, but I do not think so. The chances are, you will have to prepare for a struggle, in which case the notice should go up promptly on the morning of the 25th. Of course you will win, and win easier than you suppose, owing to the present condition of markets.[4]

1. What reason did Carnegie give for refusing to recognize the union?

2. How did Carnegie feel workers' wages would be affected?

3. How did Carnegie feel improvements at Homestead would affect workers' wages?

4. To what fact did Carnegie attribute the payment of higher wages at the Homestead plant?

5. What did Carnegie warn Frick would happen?

[4]Correspondence from Andrew Carnegie to Henry Clay Frick, 10 June 1892, in *The Inside History of the Carnegie Steel Company*.

Name ____________________

Date ____________________

Part B.

When a strike loomed large in 1892, Henry Clay Frick, the manager of the Homestead mills, hired the Pinkerton National Detective Agency to act as special deputies and protect Carnegie Steel Corporation property. Read the following excerpt from a letter written by Frick to Robert A. Pinkerton outlining the agreement, and answer the questions.

Pittsburgh, Pa. June 2, 1892

Dear Sir: I am in receipt of your favor of the 22nd.

We will want 300 guards for service at our Homestead mills as a measure of prevention against inteferrence [sic] with our plan to start the operation of the works on July 6, 1892.

The only trouble we anticipate is that an attempt will be made to prevent such of our men, with whom we will by that time have made satisfactory arrangements, from going to work and possibly some demonstration of violence upon the part of those whose places have been filled, or most likely by an element which is usually attracted to such scenes for the purpose of stirring up trouble.

We are not desirous that the men you send shall be armed unless the occasion properly calls for such a measure later on for the protection of our employees or property. We shall wish these guards to be placed upon our property and there to remain unless called into other service by the civil authorities to meet an emergency that is not likely to arise. . . .

We think absolute secrecy essential in the movement of these men so that no demonstration can be made while they are en route. . . .

As soon as your men are upon the premises we will notify the sheriff and ask that they be deputized either at once or immediately upon an ontbreak [sic] of such a character as to render such a step desirable. . . . [5]

1. What did Frick request of the Pinkerton Agency?

2. What type of trouble did Frick anticipate and by whom?

3. Were the detective guards to be armed? Why or why not?

4. What demand did Frick make of the Pinkertons in regards to their arrival?

5. What would happen once the Pinkertons arrived on mill property?

[5]Testimony of Henry C. Frick, *U.S. Senate Report No. 1280*, Exhibit C., November 23, 1892.

Name ______________________

Date ______________________

The Battle

Part A.

Read the following account of the arrival of the Pinkerton detectives at the Homestead Works and the battle which followed, and answer the questions. This excerpt is from a young college student, John W. Holway, who was employed as a Pinkerton guard.

Holway's Testimony

Now I could not tell by looking the men over who was experienced and who was not, but there were 30 or 40 men who had been in previous strikes, always in Pinkerton's employ, so far as I could learn. . . . These men were the chief actors down there at Homestead. They were the men who, after the captain had left us, kept us from being killed. If not for their presence I believe all the men would have jumped overboard. . . . There were also regular detectives. During this firing there was a second battle. I was out of sight, but there were cracks of rifles, and our men replied with a regular fusilade. It kept up for ten minutes, bullets flying around as thick as hail, and men coming in shot and covered with blood. These detectives were about the only men that kept us from being killed. . . . A good many of the men were thoroughly demoralized. They put on life-preservers and jumped under the tables and had no control over themselves whatever. Through the rest of the day there was this second battle when the strikers started the firing. There seemed to be sharpshooters picking us off. At first they fired straight at us, but after awhile they fired through the aisles on the side, and they would shoot men who thought they were safe. The bullets would come, zip, and you would hear some man yell, and you would know they were not cautious. There were sharpshooters picking us off all day, and about 12 o'clock barrels of burning oil were floating around the bank to burn us up, to compel us to go on the wharf and there shoot us down, but they didn't succeed because the oil was taken up by the water, and at about 1 o'clock a cannon was fired by the strikers.

Now, this cannon we supposed, directly we heard it, was fired to hit us below the water line and sink our boat, but the cannon did not hit us at all hardly. It was kept up all afternoon. There was one shot came through the roof around me, through some cots, struck the wall and bounded out there, and one man picked it up. . . . At about 3 o'clock we heard something; we thought was a cannon, but it was dynamite. . . . It partially wrecked the other boat. A stick of it fell near me. . . . Most of the men were for surrender at this time [three o'clock], but the old detectives held out and said, "If you surrender you will be shot down like dogs; the best thing is to stay here." We could not cut our barges loose because there was a fall below, where we would be sunk. We were deserted by our captains and by our tug, and left there to be shot. . . . [6]

1. How did Holway characterize his fellow guards?

2. What did Holway say was his biggest fear?

[6]Testimony of John W. Holway, 18 November 1892, U.S. Senate Report 1280.

Name ____________________

Date ____________________

3. Why did Holway feel abandoned?

4. How did Holway characterize the battle?

5. Why didn't the Pinkertons cut the barges loose?

6. What was the general feeling among the Pinkertons by three o'clock?

Part B.

Read the following account of the arrival of the Pinkerton detectives at the Homestead Works and the battle which followed, and answer the questions. This excerpt is from Captain Rodgers, whose towboats brought the Pinkertons' barge to the Homestead wharf.

Captain Rodgers' Testimony

" . . . The men talked . . . of going to Carnegie to act as watchmen and seemed to have no idea of being engaged in a work of danger. On the way up from Davis island dam they seemed more intent on getting something to eat and bunking than anything else. Two-thirds of the men were asleep until the firing on the boats commenced near Homestead.

"Everything was quiet at the lock and nothing seemed of an unusual character until we were within about two miles of Homestead when we heard many whistles blowing, which impressed us with the idea we were expected. As we neared Homestead daylight was breaking and we could see the crowd gathering on the Homestead shore. . . .

"The first crowd attacked and tried to stop our tying up and putting out a stage plank. As they came it was something like a charge over the river bank, with the evident intent to get on the barges. They got on the stage and were met by the Pinkerton men. . . . another Pinkerton man was endeavoring to keep the crowd back with an oar, the man lying on the landing stage fired the first shot at [Captain Hines]—I mean the first shot that did any damage—wounding him in the thigh.

"We then put out our stage, and the firing ceased with the exception of an occasional shot until we left to go to Port Perry with the wounded. Our time and theirs the next two hours was spent in taking care of the wounded.

"The arms that the Pinkerton men had were sent in advance, and were put on the boats with other stores before they arrived. On the way up, after the firing commenced, they unpacked the arms, and were engaged in it during the firing. . . . [7]

[7]"Captain Rodgers Repeats the Tale of the Ill-Fated Expedition," *The Pittsburgh Leader,* 10 July 1892.

Name ______________________

Date ______________________

1. What did Captain Rogers say most of the men on the barges believed their task would be?

2. When were the men on the barges alerted that there would be trouble?

3. What did the first crowd try to do?

4. Why did Captain Rogers abandon the barge?

5. If the Pinkertons were to be unarmed, as stated in Frick's letter to the detective agency, why were guns on board?

When the Circus Came to Town

Objectives

- To discuss the life and times of P. T. Barnum
- To explore Barnum's influence on the development of attendance at the circus as a cultural activity
- To examine and interpret photographic examples of circus life

Notes to the Teacher

In 1810, Phineas Taylor Barnum was born in Bethel, Connecticut. Barnum would come to be known as the "King of Hype and Humbug." By the time Barnum was fifteen, he was already an experienced salesman and promoter. He sold tickets to sporting events, carnivals, and theatrical performances. By the time he was thirty, he had established himself as the head of a traveling company of acrobats, circus performers, freaks, and wild animals, with which he toured the eastern United States. In 1840, he bought and reopened the American Museum in New York City, where he exhibited a feegee [sic] mermaid, a bearded lady, fossils, and natural history displays.

When Barnum discovered Tom Thumb, he advertised him as the world's smallest man and toured the United States with him. In 1844, Barnum left for Europe on a series of tours, with Thumb as his star attraction. In 1850, Barnum brought Jenny Lind, the Swedish Nightingale, to the United States on a triumphant tour. Barnum was the first theatrical promoter in the United States to hype his performers. Beginning in 1871, he toured the United States and Canada by train with the "Greatest Show on Earth." Barnum's show always had the "biggest," "most ferocious," "most exotic," and "most dangerous" exhibits. Merging with the circus run by his most prominent rivals, the Bailey Brothers, Barnum created the Barnum and Bailey Brothers Circus. Perhaps one of the most famous of Barnum's exhibits was Jumbo, the world's largest African elephant, which Barnum obtained for the price of $10,000 from the Royal Zoological Society in London. Brought to America by ship, Jumbo quickly became one of Barnum's most popular attractions, even after his death. Killed by a train in Ontario, Canada, in 1885, Jumbo was stuffed by a taxidermist and continued to tour with the Barnum circus. Later the preserved elephant was exhibited at Barnum Hall of Tufts College. Barnum was first elected a trustee of Tufts College in 1851 and served until 1857, when he informed the college that his business demanded his full attention. Barnum maintained a home in Connecticut all his life and continued to support Tufts College. He contributed money for the construction of the Barnum Museum of Natural History, later Barnum Hall, which was to house his collection of oddities and mounted circus animals, including the preserved remains of Jumbo. Barnum died in Bridgeport, Connecticut, in 1891. A fire later destroyed most of Barnum Hall and its contents, including Jumbo.

In this lesson, students discuss the life of P. T. Barnum and examine and interpret photographs of circus life. Students conclude by examining and interpreting a poster advertising one of the circus's European tours and comparing it to modern advertisements for theatrical events.

Reminder to Teachers

- Decide if the appropriate primary sources analysis worksheets from the appendix will be used in this lesson.
- Assign those sections of the basal textbook that are relevant to this lesson.

Procedure

1. Ask if students have ever been to the circus. Ask for some examples of descriptive terms which are associated with the circus (*ringmaster, three rings, trapeze artists, elephants, high wire acts*). Explain that the circus was often the most exciting thing to occur in small-town America during the late nineteenth and early twentieth century. The arrival of the circus was an event anticipated for weeks by children and adults. Explain that circuses traveled a circuit as ice shows and rock groups do today. Using the Notes to the Teacher, discuss the impact of P. T. Barnum on entertainment.

Ask students for examples of what might be considered "hype and humbug" today (*professional wrestling, the Super Bowl, rock concerts*).

2. Divide the class into small groups of three or four. Distribute one photo from **Handout 5** and one copy of **Handout 29,** the photograph analysis worksheet from the appendix, to each group. Additional copies of the photos and analysis sheet will be needed if there are more than four groups. Have students examine the photos and complete the analysis sheet. Using the photos and the analysis sheets, have each group write a short (one hundred words) description of the circus life as portrayed in the photo. Have students share their descriptions with the class.

3. Distribute **Handout 6** and a copy of **Handout 30**, the poster analysis worksheet, to students. Explain that the Barnum and Bailey Circus traveled all around the world. This poster was for an appearance in England. Consider making an overhead transparency of the poster for use in analysis. Have students examine and analyze the poster, and make a list on an overhead transparency or the chalkboard of the items which appear in the poster that are associated with the circus. Have students compare the items with what might appear in a poster for a modern form of entertainment—a concert, ice show, or movie.

4. To conclude, have students imagine they were alive at the turn of the century and the circus has just left town. Instruct students to write a letter to a friend in a neighboring city, describing some of the things that appeared at the circus. Have students share their letters.

Extension Activities

1. Have students design a poster for a modern entertainment event. The design should mirror the format used by Barnum in advertising his circus. Have students share their posters with the class. Display selected posters in the classroom.

2. Have selected students conduct an Internet search for additional information about P. T. Barnum and the Barnum and Bailey Circuses. Students might want to research the Rollins College in Florida, which offers a major in Clowning.

3. Have students view the A&E Network's film *Barnum*, which is available for rental or purchase.

Name ____________________

Date ____________________

The Greatest Show on Earth

The following photographs were taken during the last half of the nineteenth century. They illustrate circus life in America during that time period. Examine the photographs and complete **Handout 29,** the Photograph Analysis Worksheet.

Fig. 2.1.

Fig. 2.1. Ticket wagon, Barnum & Bailey, 1888. Circus World Museum, Baraboo, Wisconsin. Used by permission.

Name ___________________________

Date ___________________________

Fig. 2.2.

Fig. 2.2. Horse-drawn tableau wagon. From the Collection of Howard Tibbals. Used by permission.

Name ______________________

Date ______________________

Fig. 2.3.

Fig. 2.4.

Fig. 2.3. Negative #16,382. Barnum elephants, Old Home Week. Town House Square. Courtesy Peabody Essex Museum.

Fig. 2.4. Side show talker and snake charmer, Barnum & Bailey, 1888. Circus World Museum, Baraboo, Wisconsin. Used by permission.

Name ______________________

Date ______________________

Circus Advertisement

Large lithographic posters were used to advertise theatrical and entertainment events at the end of the nineteenth century. This example of an advertising poster was used by P. T. Barnum to promote an appearance by his circus in England. Use **Handout 30,** the Poster Analysis Worksheet, to examine the poster below. Make a list of the items associated with the circus, which appear in the poster. Be prepared to compare the circus poster with one advertising a modern entertainment event.

Fig. 2.5.

Fig. 2.5. Cover of *Advance-Courier* for the 1889–90 Barnum and Bailey appearance in London. Historical Collections, Bridgeport Public Library.

Recording History through Different Eyes

Objectives

- To examine how different cultures view similar events
- To discuss the importance of the accuracy of historical records

Notes to the Teacher

Primary source documents may take many forms. They may be written, drawn, photographed, and printed. Cultures with no written language, as was the case with most nineteenth-century Native Americans, would have relied on oral tradition to pass down information about important events to their descendants. After the Battle of the Little Big Horn, Native American versions of the battle were recorded using interviews and drawings, which provide us with fairly accurate accounts. Soldiers serving in the army on the Plains often were illiterate. Some, however, recorded events in their journals.

In June 1876, George Armstrong Custer and more than 260 cavalrymen died at the Battle of the Little Big Horn. As a result, hundreds of soldiers were posted to frontier forts to reinforce the Army's struggling campaign against the Native American tribes of the northern plains. One of those soldiers, William F. Zimmer, a German immigrant, served in the army during the waning days of the Civil War. At the end of that conflict he worked as a farmer for ten years before reenlisting in the regular army, three months after the Battle of the Little Big Horn. Between March 1 and December 31, 1877, Zimmer kept a journal of his activities. During this time, he witnessed the end of the army's campaign against the Sioux and the final confrontation between the army and the Nez Perce under the leadership of Chief Joseph.

Red Horse was a Miniconjou warrior who was persuaded to relate his version of the events that occurred at the Battle of the Little Big Horn. Acting Assistant Surgeon Dr. Charles E. McChesney, who was assigned to the Cheyenne River Reservation where Red Horse was being confined, convinced him to prepare a series of forty-two drawings that depicted the battle.

In this lesson, students read journal entries written by William F. Zimmer and examine and interpret a selection of drawings by Red Horse. Students create a drawing to represent Zimmer's journal entry in the method of Red Horse.

Reminder to Teachers

- Decide if the appropriate primary sources analysis worksheets from the appendix will be used in this lesson.
- Assign those sections of the basal textbook that are relevant to this lesson.

Procedure

1. Ask students if they have ever kept a diary or journal. Ask what types of events they would record (*special events, such as birthdays and graduations; daily events and occurrences; observations on their family and friends, and events occurring around them*). Ask students how they would record these events if they did not have a written language (*draw pictures*). Distribute **Handout 7** and explain the circumstances of William F. Zimmer's journal writing, using the information in the Notes to the Teacher. Divide the students into groups of three or four, and have them read the handout. Ask the value of Zimmer's journal. (*It provides an accurate record of service in the army during the Indian Wars; it is very detailed and descriptive.*) Ask why Zimmer kept a journal (*to record his thoughts and observations so that he could remember them and tell his family about them*).
2. Explain that some cultures have no written language and its members must rely on oral tradition or pictographs to record historical events. Distribute one part of **Handout 8** to each group. In a large class, more than one group will have the same part. Have each group examine and interpret the action portrayed in the drawing.

Suggested Responses:

Fig. 3.1. *Soldiers are attacking the Indian village.*

Fig. 3.2. *The Cavalry is being forced back as indicated by their being pushed back over their footprints.*

Fig. 3.3. *The Sioux are fighting Custer.*

Fig. 3.4. *Custer's column is fighting the Indians.*

Fig. 3.5. *The Sioux are killed by Custer's army.*

Have each group share its drawing and interpretation. Ask if the drawings were as accurate and descriptive as Zimmer's journal. Provide each group with a large sheet of paper (the unprinted side of wrapping paper or butcher paper is best) and ask the groups to create a drawing that interprets Zimmer's diary entry. Have them display and share their drawings with the class.

3. Conclude the lesson by having each group prepare a short journal entry describing a recent event in school or the students' school day. Have groups exchange journal entries. Have students illustrate the journal entry in a similar fashion to that of Red Horse. Have students share and evaluate the accuracy of each group's drawing.

Extension Activities

1. Have students examine other cultures' methods of recording their history, including hieroglyphics, wall paintings, etc. and report to the class.
2. Have students look at newspaper, magazine, and television accounts of the same story and compare and contrast the way in which different individuals record the same event.

Name ______________________

Date ______________________

An Enlisted Man's Journal

William F. Zimmer, a soldier in the U.S. army during the Indian Wars, kept a journal during the year immediately following the Battle of the Little Big Horn. Below is an excerpt from that journal. Read the selection carefully, and be prepared to discuss it.

August 1, 1877

Weather pleasant. About 4 P.M. we reached the Little Missouri River, where we left the Sioux trail on the 14th of July. After crossing and going up a mile we went in camp for the night. We had not been in camp but a short time, when 66 more Crow warriors came to us down the numerous ravines that lead to the river, in single file with their feathers flying and they yelling like fiends of Hell. They were in charge of an infantry officer. They went in camp along with the other Indians that came to us last night. After supper had been got away with, about one hundred Indians mounted their ponies, first having fixed their toilets in war paint, and adorned their head and hair with feathers. Also, the mane and tail of their ponies, and those having white ponies (which are very plenty amongst them) they daub red paint on so as to look as though they had been wounded. They formed a half-mile ring around our camp and began to ride on a brisk trot, at the same time singing and shouting at the top of their voices, and those that were not mounted stood in groups around the ring indulging in the same kind of vocal music. They have no flags, but long stained rods on which they have long streamers of feathers. On some there is scalps cut in long strips, with the hair hanging and fluttering in the breeze as they rode around at the same time swinging their rifles, tomahawks or knives over their heads in a fantastic manner. They kept this up for half an hour, then going to their camp they commenced their medicine making, which they kept up until 12 midnight. This war dance or jamboree which I have been trying to explain, would beat Barnum's Hippodrome all to pieces [P. T. Barnum's Greatest Show on Earth]. Their war headdresses are made in different styles, but the most common are a buckskin turban, steamers of the same which hang nearly down to the ground. The outside of the turban is beaded, & in the inside the feathers are fastened in an upright position. On the streamers, they are fastened in such a way so as to flutter when they are riding fast. . . . The feathers that are principally used are those of the eagle and wild turkey. Indians are very fond of bright and gaudy colors, and if they see any trinket which they like they will have it regardless of cost, if they have the price of it in their possession. And jewelry they all wear. Of course, it's nothing but brass or German silver. Some of them will have a cord around their necks filled with all kinds of stuff just so it shines. I have seen some with rings on all of their fingers—not only one on a finger, but 3 and 4 on each. And for earrings, it's awful. They will be from 2 to 2½ inches across and from 3 to 4 in each ear, one above the other. And the holes in the outer edge of their ears are as large as an eyelet in a shoe. Besides the weight of these rings, they have from 2 to 3 ounces of trinkets, such as fancy little shells, elk tusks, and large beads, all suspended from their ears. (Perhaps it would be as well here to give you their mode of dress. On their feet they wear moccasins altogether, either made of buffalo or deerskin, according to the weather. On their body they wear a shirt, leggins & a breechclout. Then, according to the severity of the weather, they either wear a blanket or a robe about the body. Their heads are generally bare. They are more apt to buy a hat of the trader to keep the sun off, than a cap for winter use. The squaws seldom ever wear anything else than a piece of calico about their heads. Their bodily dress is much the same as the male, with an additional short skirt made of a blanket. In fact, all their wearing apparel is made of blankets except shirts, which are invariably red flannel. They would go to Hell after

Name ____________________

Date ____________________

a red blanket if they couldn't get it outside. The way the leggins are made is this: They take a piece of blanket wide enough to leave a selvage 4 inches wide on the outside of the leg, which is cut into fringe. They sometimes make a ghastly looking cloak with a hood to it, which they fringe wherever they can put it on. They never pretend to wash anything in the clothing line, though they are quite fond of bathing when the water is warm. Yet I doubt whether they do it for cleanliness. I rather think it's done for coolness.)[1]

[1] William F. Zimmer, *Frontier Soldier: An Enlisted Man's Journal of the Sioux and Nez Perce Campaigns, 1877*, edited and annotated by Jerome A. Greene (Helena, Mont.: The Montana Historical Society Press, 1998), 89–92.

Name ______________________

Date ______________________

A Native American's View of the Battle of the Little Big Horn

The Native Americans of the northern Plains were a people for whom an oral tradition was very important. Not having a written language, they could only record the past by passing down accounts of events from generation to generation. In 1881, a Miniconjou warrior, Red Horse, at the urging of Dr. Charles E. McChesney, an army surgeon attached to the Cheyenne River Reservation in South Dakota, produced a set of forty-two drawings illustrating the Battle of the Little Big Horn. Examine each of the following five drawings, and write a brief description of what each portrays. Be prepared to share your description in class.

Fig. 3.1.

Fig. 3.1. National Anthropological Archives, Smithsonian Institution/46,000-D.

Name ______________________

Date ______________________

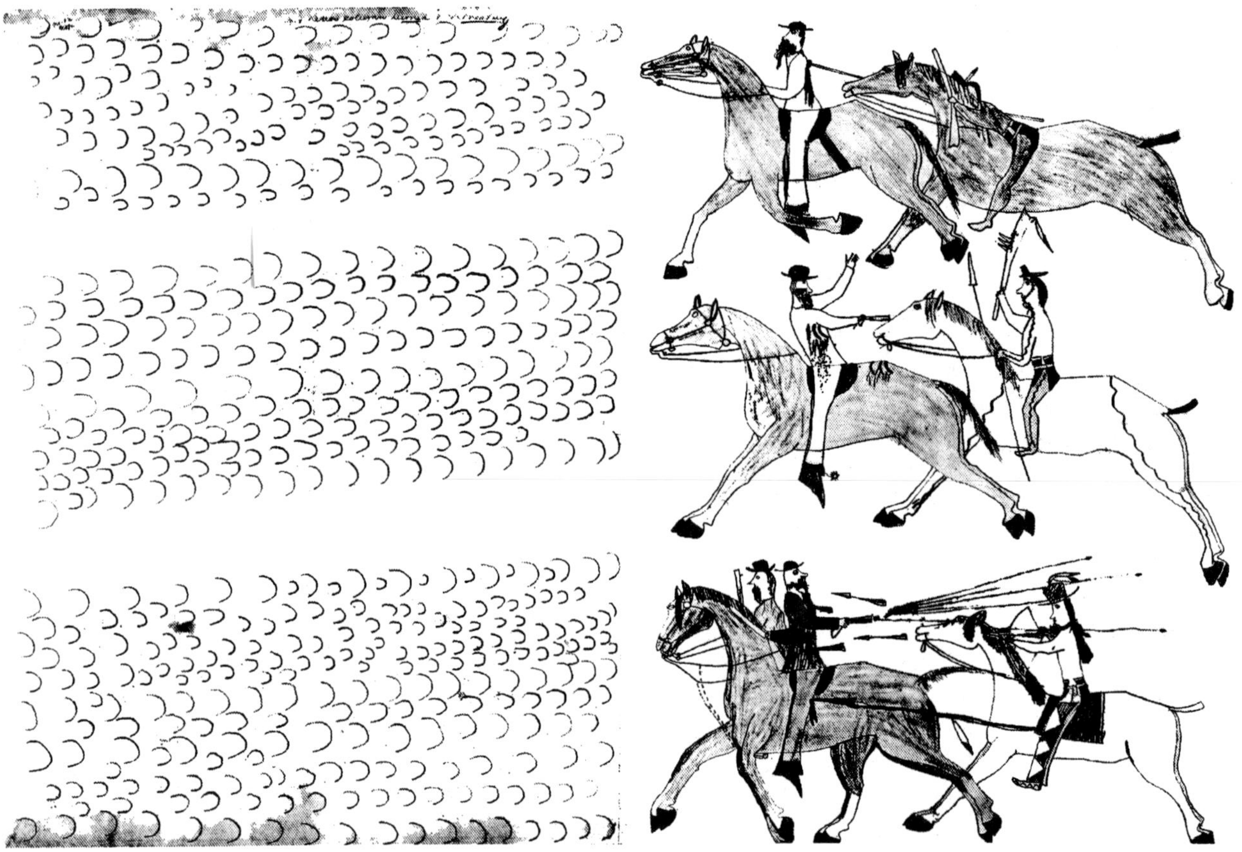

Fig. 3.2.

Fig. 3.2. National Anthropological Archives, Smithsonian Institution/46,999-G.

Name ______________________

Date ______________________

Fig. 3.3.

Fig. 3.3. National Anthropological Archives, Smithsonian Institution/47,000.

Name ____________________

Date ____________________

Fig. 3.4.

Fig. 3.4. National Anthropological Archives, Smithsonian Institution/47,000-A.

Name ___________________________

Date ___________________________

Fig. 3.5.

Fig. 3.5. National Anthropological Archives, Smithsonian Institution/47,000-H.

Lesson 4—Immigration

The Chinese Exclusion Act

Objectives

- To assess the development of anti-Chinese bias in America during the latter half of the nineteenth century
- To examine the passage of anti-Chinese legislation by Congress in the 1880s

Notes to the Teacher

Throughout our history, immigrants from dozens of countries have entered the United States seeking freedom and prosperity. Hard-working and diligent, these newcomers often lived under the harshest, most difficult conditions and often performed jobs that the average American refused. Viewed by Americans as a threat to their livelihood, immigrants were often subject to harassment and abuse. Signs which read "No Irish Need Apply" (NINA) often appeared in the windows of businesses in cities along the Atlantic seaboard. Anti-immigrant groups, such as the Know-Nothings, became political powers in some sections of the United States. It was not surprising that the Chinese became a target of anti-immigrant bias during the late nineteenth century.

The acquisition of California during the Mexican War and the discovery of gold at Sutter's Mill in 1848 marked the beginning of the real settlement of the West. Thousands of would-be miners poured into the Sierra Nevadas in search of gold. While North America, South America, and Europe provided the bulk of the miners, some, like the Sydney Ducks (known for their brutal gang activities), came from as far away as Australia. The Chinese began to arrive during the Gold Rush, and by 1860, large numbers of Chinese were providing cheap labor for the construction of the western end of the transcontinental railroad. So many came that by the 1870s and 1880s American workers found themselves competing with Asian laborers for jobs. Bowing to pressure from the newly organized labor unions, Congress attempted to limit the number of Chinese workers immigrating to America by passing the Chinese Exclusion Act in 1882.

In this lesson, students read and analyze three sources: an example of a visual which illustrates the anti-Chinese bias in America at the end of the nineteenth century; an excerpt from the Knights of Labor pamphlet, which warns of the dangers of allowing the Chinese to continue to enter the United States; and excerpts from the Chinese Exclusion Act of 1882.

Reminder to Teachers

- Decide if the appropriate primary sources analysis worksheets from the appendix will be used in this lesson.
- Assign those sections of the basal textbook that are relevant to this lesson.

Procedure

1. Ask if students know what is required to allow an immigrant to enter the United States (*must have valid documents from his or her native country; must enter under the current immigration laws; may not be a criminal or mentally ill; may be granted refugee status depending on the circumstances in his or her native land*). Explain that before 1900, the United States encouraged immigrants to enter the country in order to provide workers for America's growing industries and settlers for the vast western lands. Explain that some immigrant groups were abused and mistreated. Briefly discuss the conditions that confronted the Irish when they came to the United States beginning around 1825. Lesson 4, "The Coming of the Irish," in *Primary Sources in U.S. History: Antebellum America and Civil War, 1840–1865* may be used to discuss the problems facing Irish immigrants fleeing the potato famine in the mid-1840s. Ask students who the Know-Nothings were (*a group of nativists who supported public policies that opposed the admission of Catholics, Jews, and other immigrants to the United States.*)
2. Explain that the Chinese began to arrive in the western United States at the time of the Gold Rush. They worked at diggings for other miners and operated restaurants and laundries. Later they worked on the construction of the Union Pacific half of the transcontinental railroad. Explain that an

anti-Chinese movement began in California after the Civil War. Ask students why bias developed against the Chinese. (*They worked for lower wages than others, sent most of their money back to China, dressed differently, frequently did not speak English, and practiced a different religion than most Americans.*)

3. Distribute **Handout 9.** Have students examine part A and complete the analysis questions. Review students' responses.

   Suggested Responses:

   1. *The Chinese are threats to Americans and would resort to violence.*
   2. *to illustrate the cover of a "pennie-dreadful"*
   3. *The message is both verbal and visual. The Chinese are portrayed as thugs who have tied "white" Americans to stakes and are prepared to set them on fire.*
   4. *The intended audience was young men and those whose jobs and livelihoods might be threatened by the Chinese.*
   5. *The stereotypes included Chinese dressed in "pajamas" and the wearing of the que.*
   6. *They portrayed the Chinese in a threatening and menacing way.*

4. Explain that labor unions were being organized for the first time during the 1880s and 1890s. Have students read part B and complete the questions for discussion. Review students' responses.

   Suggested Responses:

   1. *laundry*
   2. *Their labor took "bread from the mouths of our women." The Chinese would work for lower wages and returned nothing to the economy or trade of the country.*
   3. *It appealed to those things which most Americans believed were important.*
   4. *because they were hard workers*
   5. *They had an untiring industrial ability, an unsurpassed staying power, and a degree of patience which no other nation could pretend to equal.*

5. Explain that by the 1880s, anti-Chinese bias had become a major force in the politics of western America. Lobbyists in Congress demanded the passage of a Chinese exclusion law. In 1880, the first restrictions on Chinese immigration were enacted. Two years later, the Congress passed the Chinese Exclusion Act. Have students read part C and complete the questions for discussion. Review students' responses.

   Suggested Responses:

   1. *if it affected the interests of the United States or endangered the good order of the country*
   2. *Chinese laborers*
   3. *Chinese subjects and Chinese laborers who were already in the United States were allowed free passage.*
   4. *The government promised to secure for them the rights, privileges, immunities, and exemptions that other citizens or subjects enjoy and that the treaty entitles to them.*
   5. *ten years*
   6. *The coming of Chinese laborers to the United States was suspended.*
   7. *could not land or permit to land any Chinese laborers*
   8. *a $500 fine for each laborer and up to one year in prison*
   9. *any Chinese who entered the United States before November 17, 1880, or within ninety days of that date*
   10. *a certificate including the following information: name, title, official rank, age, height, physical peculiarities, occupation/profession, residence in China*
   11. *They would be deported.*
   12. *Chinese diplomats would not be affected.*
   13. *They were denied citizenship.*
   14. *any skilled and unskilled laborers or Chinese employed in mining*

6. Conclude by asking students to give examples of modern immigrant groups who have faced some of the same bias as the Chinese (*"boat people" from Southeast Asia, immigrants from Africa and the Middle East, immigrants from Central and South America*). Direct students to find examples of this in newspapers and magazines. Have students write a letter to the editor of their local newspaper describing the contributions of immigrants to American society. Pick selected students to share their letters.

Extension Activities

1. Have students research and report on the contributions of Chinese immigrants to American society.
2. Have a member of the local Chinese community speak to the class about the problems confronting recent immigrants.
3. Have students do further research and report to the class about the "pennie-dreadfuls." Suggest using the Web site of the Stanford University Library (http://www-sul.stanford.edu/depts/dp/pennies/1880_chinese.html) as a starting point.

Name ____________________

Date ____________________

Visual Images and the Chinese Exclusion

Part A.

An anti-Chinese bias developed during the last half of the nineteenth century. Dime novels were the reading material of choice for most Americans. The simple, often repetitious plots and colorful illustrations captured the eye of the average American, particularly young men and boys. The tendency of writers to stereotype the characters depicted, as they did in the case of their portrayal of the Chinese as individuals who spent their time in opium dens and abducting white women who would become addicted to the drug and be forced into prostitution, contributed to the development of an anti-Chinese bias in America. Examine the following example of a dime novel cover, and complete the analysis questions.

The Chinese Dwarf seemed to be having everything his own way. The wood was rapidly piled around Old King Brady and Harry. The other Chinamen watched all these preparations with stolid indifference. There seemed no hope of escape.

Fig. 4.1.

Fig. 4.1. *The Bradys and the Chinese Dwarf; or, The "Que Hunter" of the Barbary Coast, by a New-York Detective.* http://www-sul.stanford.edu/depts/dp/pennies/1880_chinese.html. Department of Special Collections, Stanford University Libraries.

Name ______________________

Date ______________________

1. What is the message of the illustration?

2. What is its purpose?

3. Is the message more verbal or visual? Explain your answer.

4. Who do you think was the intended audience?

5. What stereotypic images appear in the illustration?

6. How did illustrations like this encourage anti-Chinese bias?

Name ______________________

Date ______________________

Part B.

The early labor movements in America, such as the Knights of Labor, opposed the admission of Chinese immigrants to the United States on the grounds that they were taking jobs from "native" Americans. Read the following excerpt from an anti-Chinese pamphlet produced by a member of the Knights of Labor in 1878, and answer the questions that follow. Be prepared for class discussion.

China's Menace to the World

by Thomas Magee

MEN FROM CHINA come here to do LAUNDRY WORK. The Chinese Empire contains 600,000,000 (six hundred millions) inhabitants.

The supply of these men is inexhaustible.

Every one doing this work takes BREAD from the mouths of OUR WOMEN.

So many have come of late, that to keep at work, they are obliged to cut prices.

And now, we appeal to the public, asking them will they be partners to a deal which is only one of their many onward marches in CRUSHING OUT THE INDUSTRIES OF OUR COUNTRY from our people by grasping them themselves. Will you oblige the AMERICAN LAUNDRIES to CUT THE WAGES OF THEIR PEOPLE by giving your patronage to the CHINAMEN?

We invite you to give a thorough investigation of the STEAM LAUNDRY BUSINESS OF THE COUNTRY; in doing so you will find that not only does it GIVE EMPLOYMENT TO A VAST NUMBER OF WOMEN, but a great field of labor is opened to a great number of mechanics of all kinds whose wages are poured back into the trade of the country.

If this understandable element "THE CHINESE EMIGRANTS" are not stopped coming here, we have no alternative but that we will have California and the Pacific Slope's experience, and the end will be that our industries will be absorbed UNLESS we live down to their animal life.

We say in conclusion that the CHINAMAN is a labor consumer of our country without the adequate returns of prosperity to our land as is given by the labor of our people to our glorious country.

Our motto should be:

OUR COUNTRY, OUR PEOPLE, OUR GOD, AND OUR NATIVE LAND.

Pioneer Laundry Workers Assembly, K. of L. Washington, D.C. . . .

. . . China is no longer shut; China is open, and China's only grievance may be that the world, in its turn, may build an anti-Chinese legal wall against the entrance of her innumerable industrial armies. The world does not know much about China yet; it will soon, however, make more of her acquaintance. She has been hidden in the night of exclusion, oriental sleep, and mental stagnation; she is emerging into the daylight of progress, and toward an activity such as the modern world has never seen. China has been ignorantly despised, but China is worthy of all respect. She is quickly throwing off the clogs of her progress, and is rapidly coming up with the open world in the race of life, with advantages in her favor that cannot well be surpassed. The man who can run for a few minutes in a short race, and make very

Name ______________________

Date ______________________

fast time, is not the equal of him who can run all day. The Chinese are all-day runners, and those who compete with them will need to rise early and sit up late. China has untiring industrial ability, unsurpassed staying powers, and a degree of patience which no other nation can pretend to equal. Friend and enemy of China should know these facts. Few do know them.[1]

1. What job did the Chinese perform?

2. Why did the Knights of Labor oppose the entrance of more Chinese to America?

3. What is the appeal of the motto "Our country, our people, our God, and our native land"?

4. Why did Magee say that the Chinese were to be respected?

5. Why did Magee compare the Chinese to an all-day runner?

[1]Thomas Magee, *China's Menace to the World: From the Forum to the Public*, 1878. Library of Congress, Rare Book and Special Collections Division, Daniel A. P. Murray Pamphlets Collection.

Name ______________________

Date ______________________

Part C.

In 1880, the U.S. Congress approved a treaty with China that restricted the immigration of Chinese to America. In 1882, Congress passed the Chinese Exclusion Act, which limited Chinese immigration to the United States. Read the following excerpts, and complete the questions for discussion.

Treaty Regulating Immigration from China
November 17, 1880

ART. I. Whenever in the opinion of the Government of the United States, the coming of Chinese laborers to the United States, or their residence therein, affects or threatens to affect the interests of that country, or to endanger the good order of the said country or of any locality within the territory thereof, the Government of China agrees that the Government of the United States may regulate, limit, or suspend such coming or residence, but may not absolutely prohibit it. The limitation or suspension shall be reasonable and shall apply only to Chinese who may go to the United States as laborers, other classes not being included in the limitations. Legislation taken in regard to Chinese laborers will be of such a character only as is necessary to enforce the regulation, limitation or suspension of immigration, and immigrants shall not be subject to personal maltreatment or abuse.

ART. II. Chinese subjects, whether proceeding to the United States as teachers, students, merchants, or from curiosity, together with their body and household servants, and Chinese laborers who are now in the United States, shall be allowed to go and come of their own free will and accord, and shall be accorded all the rights, privileges, immunities and exemptions which are accorded to the citizens and subjects of the most favored nation.

ART. III. If Chinese laborers, or Chinese of any other class, now either permanently or temporarily residing in the territory of the United States, meet with ill treatment at the hands of any other persons, the Government of the United States will exert all its power to devise measures for their protection and to secure to them the same rights, privileges, immunities and exemptions as may be enjoyed by the citizens or subjects of the most favored nation, and to which they are entitled by treaty. . . .[2]

1. Under what circumstances would Chinese immigration be restricted?

2. To whom did the restrictions apply?

[2]"Treaty Regulating Immigration from China," 17 November 1880, in *Treaties, Conventions, International Acts, Protocols and Agreements between the United States of America and Other Powers*, vol. 1, comp. William M. Malloy (Washington, D.C.: Government Printing Office, 1910), 237 ff.

Name ______________________

Date ______________________

3. Who was allowed free passage to the United States?

4. How did the government promise to protect the Chinese?

Chinese Exclusion Act
May 6, 1882

An act to execute certain treaty stipulations relating to Chinese.

WHEREAS, in the opinion of the Government of the United States the coming of Chinese laborers to this country endangers the good order of certain localities within the territory thereof: Therefore,

Be it enacted, That from and after the expiration of ninety days next after the passage of this act, and until the expiration of ten years next after the passage of this act, the coming of Chinese laborers to the United States shall be . . . suspended; and during such suspension it shall not be lawful for any Chinese laborer to come, or, having so come after the expiration of said ninety days, to remain within the United States.

SEC. 2. That the master of any vessel who shall knowingly bring within the United States on such vessel, and land or permit to be landed, any Chinese laborer, from any foreign port or place, shall be deemed guilty of a misdemeanor, and on conviction thereof shall be punished by a fine of not more than five hundred dollars for each and every such Chinese laborer so brought, and may be also imprisoned for a term not exceeding one year.

SEC. 3. That the two foregoing sections shall not apply to Chinese laborers who were in the United States on the seventeenth day of November, eighteen hundred and eighty, or who shall have come into the same before the expiration of ninety days next after the passage of this act. . . .

SEC. 6. That in order to the faithful execution of articles one and two of the treaty in this act before mentioned, every Chinese person other than a laborer who may be entitled by said treaty and this act to come within the United States, and who shall be about to come to the United States, shall be identified as so entitled by the Chinese Government in each case, such identity to be evidenced by a certificate issued under the authority of said government, and which certificate shall be in the English language or (if not in the English language) accompanied by a translation into English, stating such right to come, and which certificate shall state the name, title, or official rank, if any, the age, height, and all physical peculiarities, former and present occupation or profession and place of residence in China of the person to whom the certificate is issued and that such person is entitled conformably to the treaty in this act mentioned to come within the United States. . . .

Name ________________________

Date ________________________

SEC. 12. That no Chinese person shall be permitted to enter the United States by land without producing to the proper office of customs the certificate in this act required of Chinese persons seeking to land from a vessel. Any Chinese person found unlawfully within the United States shall be caused to be removed therefrom to the country from whence he came, by direction of the President of the United States, and at the cost of the United States, after being brought before some justice, judge, or commissioner of a court of the United States and found to be one not lawfully entitled to be or remain in the United States.

SEC. 13. That this act shall not apply to diplomatic and other officers of the Chinese Government traveling upon the business of that government, whose credentials shall be taken as equivalent to the certificate in this act mentioned, and shall exempt them and their body and household servants from the provisions of this act as to other Chinese persons.

SEC. 14. That hereafter no State court or court of the United States shall admit Chinese to citizenship; and all laws in conflict with this act are hereby repealed.

SEC. 15. That the words "Chinese laborers," whenever used in this act, shall be construed to mean both skilled and unskilled laborers and Chinese employed in mining.[3]

5. For how long was the treaty to be in effect?

6. What did the treaty suspend?

7. What restrictions were placed on ship's captains?

8. What punishment could result if the ship's captains violated the terms of the treaty?

9. Who was exempt under the terms of the treaty?

10. What was required of the Chinese government to regulate any other travelers?

11. What would happen to Chinese who are in the United States illegally?

12. How did the treaty affect Chinese diplomats?

13. What was to be the citizenship status of the Chinese?

14. How did the treaty define laborers?

[3]"Chinese Exclusion Act," 6 May 1882, 22 *Stat.* 58 ff.

Lesson 5—Larger World/Diplomacy

The Annexation of Hawaii

Objectives

- To examine the circumstances leading to the annexation of Hawaii to the United States
- To assess the importance of the annexation of Hawaii to the establishment of America's position as a world power

Notes to the Teacher

For many years, the United States had been an important force in the Hawaiian Islands. New England whalers had stopped at the port of Lahaina on the island of Maui to resupply their ships. Missionaries from the United States had spread Victorian morality and Christianity among the Hawaiian people, and American ships involved in the China trade had stopped off in the islands during their long journeys across the vast Pacific. After the Civil War, American investors had established sugar and pineapple plantations in Hawaii, and profits soared during the 1890s. Russian and British interest in Hawaii prompted American sugar growers to act against the interests of the Hawaiian monarchy by declaring the islands to be an independent republic and petitioning the U.S. Congress to annex the islands.

On July 7, 1898, the U.S. Congress approved a joint resolution which annexed the Hawaiian Islands. Growing U.S. commercial interests, especially among those who grew and processed sugar, and America's need to exploit the strategic military importance of the islands, resulted in an overthrow of the legitimate monarchy of Queen Lili'uokalani in 1887. A constitutional monarch, Lili'uokalani had succeeded to the throne at the death of her brother. She ruled over vast personal lands, which the sugar interests had repeatedly attempted to purchase or lease. In 1887, the king, under pressure from American sugar interests, replaced the constitution of Hawaii with a more liberal document, which favored the sugar interests. When Lili'uokalani chose to ignore the interests of the sugar growers, they overthrew the queen and established a government that they felt would be more favorable to their interests. A provisional government was established under the direction of a Committee of Safety, with Sanford P. Dole as president. American naval forces waiting in the harbor at Honolulu came ashore to "protect" American interests. Dole and other representatives of the sugar interests submitted a draft of a treaty of annexation to President Grover Cleveland. Cleveland was thought to be more favorable to the annexation than his predecessors but refused to be rushed into submitting the treaty to Congress. Instead, he appointed an investigator to examine the revolution which Dole and Minister to Hawaii John L. Stevens had instigated. Lili'uokalani protested that the revolution had not involved any of the more than forty thousand Hawaiians who called the islands home. Cleveland addressed Congress about the problem and informed them that he believed that the provisional government was illegal and that the rightful government, that of Lili'uokalani, should be restored. He attempted to negotiate an agreement with the queen which would protect American interests and not retaliate for the actions of the sugar interests. If Lili'uokalani had agreed to restore the liberal constitution of 1887, Cleveland as president would recognize her right to rule as queen. Lili'uokalani agreed, but Sanford Dole refused to step aside. On July 4, 1894, the provisional government under Dole's leadership issued a document which created the Republic of Hawaii. The following month, the United States officially recognized the republic as an independent country. Cleveland was reluctant to use force to remove the provisional government and allowed it to be recognized but used his political power to block annexation.

The importance of the islands as a coaling and supply station would become obvious during the Spanish-American War when the American navy became involved in what was effectively a world war. In 1897, President William McKinley negotiated a new treaty with the Republic of Hawaii. This treaty acknowledged the strategic importance of Pearl Harbor to the American navy. On February 1, 1898, Dole went one step further and proclaimed Hawaii to be an American protectorate. He again requested annexation by the United States. McKinley, anxious to protect American interests abroad and realizing that he did not have the two-thirds majority needed for the passage of an annexation treaty, settled for the passage of a joint resolution, which required only a majority vote. The passage of the joint resolution created the Territory of Hawaii in 1900, and Sanford P. Dole was appointed its first governor.

In this lesson, students examine and analyze three documents associated with the annexation and draw conclusions about the importance of the annexation to America's position as a world power at the end of the nineteenth century.

Reminder to Teachers

- Decide if the appropriate primary sources analysis worksheets from the appendix will be used in this lesson.
- Assign those sections of the basal textbook that are relevant to this lesson.

Procedure

1. Display a map of the world, and ask why the Hawaiian Islands were important to the establishment of the United States as a world power. (*The islands were of economic and strategic importance to the United States; factors included the profits from sugar manufacture and the importance of coaling stations in the islands to the maintenance of the U.S. naval fleet in the Pacific.*) Distribute **Handout 10.** Discuss the background to the declaration of the Hawaiian republic as contained in the Notes to the Teacher. Have students read part A and complete the questions for discussion. Review students' responses.

   Suggested Responses:

   1. *It was the first time the United States had reached beyond the North America continent to add territory.*
   2. *Student responses should include the following: the provisional government did not have the sanction of the people either through suffrage or revolution; U.S. naval vessels were used to support the action of the provisional government; Lili'uokalani had yielded her power only because she feared the superior force of the U.S. military; members of the committee had lied about using the support of the U.S. minister and the navy; the U.S. minister to Hawaii had acted openly in support of the actions of the committee; the president had submitted the treaty to the Senate with the understanding that the U.S. diplomatic and military representatives in Hawaii had not openly promoted the overthrow of the Hawaiian government.*
   3. *He regarded it as an act of war against Hawaii; the actions of the American minister to Hawaii were undertaken without the consent or authority of the Congress.*
   4. *He proposed to restore the monarchy and power to Lili'uokalani, set up a general amnesty for all involved, and recognize the obligations of the United States to Hawaii.*
   5. *She refused to accept the terms of Cleveland's proposal.*

2. Explain that the members of the Senate of the Republic of Hawaii, the majority of whom were non-Hawaiians, voted to petition the United States for the annexation of Hawaii as an American territory. Have students read part B and list the eight points of the resolution. Review students' responses.

   Suggested Responses:

   1. *All sovereignty over the Hawaiian Islands was to be ceded to the United States and the Territory of Hawaii was to be created.*
   2. *All public, government, and crown lands were to be transferred to U.S. control.*
   3. *Existing federal laws regarding public lands were not to apply to Hawaii. Special legislation to govern the distribution of public lands would be enacted.*
   4. *All revenues from land were to be used to support the civil, military, and naval purposes of the U.S. in Hawaii.*
   5. *Local government would remain in place unless changed by the Congress.*
   6. *U.S. customs regulations would apply to all goods exported or imported in Hawaii.*
   7. *The United States would assume the public debt of Hawaii, not to exceed $4 million.*
   8. *Chinese immigration to Hawaii was prohibited, and any Chinese living in Hawaii could not move to the mainland United States.*

The resolution passed by the Senate of the Republic of Hawaii and the joint resolution of Congress supporting the annexation of the islands were almost identical documents. Ask students why they believe this happened. (*The supporters of the annexation were in close contact with the members of the republic's legislature and probably influenced the contents of the document.*)

3. Lili'uokalani, Hawaii's queen, strongly opposed the seizure and annexation of her country by the United States. Ask students for examples of some of the obstacles that she faced when she journeyed to Washington to present her views to Congress (*long journey across the Pacific and then across the country to Washington; supporters of the annexation in Congress would oppose a hearing of her views*). Have students read part C and complete the questions for discussion. Review students' responses.

Suggested Responses:

1. *Student answers should include the following: an act of wrong had been committed toward the native and part-native people of Hawaii; the treaty was an invasion on the rights of the ruling chiefs; the treaty was a violation of international rights because it prohibited Hawaii from making trade agreements with nations other than the U.S.; the treaty was a perpetuation of fraud; it was a gross act of injustice towards Lili'uokalani's rights as the legitimately selected ruler of a sovereign country.*
2. *She feared bloodshed and recognized the superior power of the American navy.*
3. *No Hawaiian citizens had served on the committee; the committee was composed of American citizens; no one had consulted with the Hawaiian people, who constituted four-fifths of the voting electorate, about the overthrow of the monarchy.*
4. *One-fourth of the land proposed to be seized was the personal property of the Hawaiian monarch and therefore not subject to sale.*
5. *Grover Cleveland, who was president at the time of annexation was first proposed*
6. *President William McKinley*

4. Conclude by having students write an essay that supports or opposes the action of the U.S. government in its seizure and annexation of the Hawaiian Islands and the destruction of its legitimate ruler, Lili'uokalani. Have selected students share their essays with the class.

Extension Activities

1. Have students research and report on the annexation of other territorial properties, such as Cuba, Puerto Rico, or Guam, that occurred in the late nineteenth century.
2. Have students research and report on other annexation questions in American history, such as Texas, Oregon, or the current question of statehood for territories, such as Puerto Rico.
3. Have students research and report on the current movement among the native people of Hawaii to split from the United States and reestablish a monarchy in the Islands.

Name ________________________

Date ________________________

Expansion into the Pacific

Part A.

In 1893, the constitutional monarchy of the island nation of Hawaii was overthrown by a group of American businessmen calling themselves the Committee of Safety. President Grover Cleveland initially supported the annexation of Hawaii because of its economic and strategic importance, but after having learned the circumstances and realities of the situation, he ordered an investigation. He appeared before Congress on December 18, 1893, to report on his findings and to recommend that the government of Hawaii be restored. Read the selection and answer the questions that follow. Be prepared for class discussion.

Grover Cleveland's Message to Congress

In my recent annual message to the Congress I briefly referred to our relations with Hawaii and expressed the intention of transmitting further information on the subject when additional advises permitted. . . .

When the present Administration entered upon its duties the Senate had under consideration a treaty providing for the annexation of the Hawaiian Islands to the territory of the United States. . . . Additional importance attached to this particular treaty of annexation, because it contemplated a departure from unbroken American tradition in providing for the addition to our territory of islands of the sea more than two thousand miles removed from our nearest coast.

These considerations might not of themselves call for interference with the completion of a treaty entered upon by a previous Administration, but it appeared from the documents . . . that the ownership of Hawaii was tendered to us by a provisional government set up to succeed the constitutional ruler of the islands, who had been dethroned, and it did not appear that such provisional government had the sanction of either popular revolution or suffrage. . . . It appeared that a so-called Committee of Safety, ostensibly the source of the revolt against the constitutional Government of Hawaii, was organized on Saturday, the 14th day of January; that on Monday, the 16th, the United States forces were landed at Honolulu from a naval vessel lying in its harbor; that on the 17th the scheme of a provisional government was perfected, and a proclamation naming its officers was on the same day prepared and read at the Government building; that immediately thereupon the United States Minister recognized the provisional government thus created. . . .

. . . it clearly appeared that there was open and undetermined an issue of fact of the most vital importance. The message of the President accompanying the treaty declared that "the overthrow of the monarchy was not in any way promoted by this Government," and in a letter to the President from the Secretary of State also submitted to the Senate with the treaty, the following message occurs: "At the time the provisional government took possession of the Government buildings no troops or officers of the United States were present or took any part whatever in the proceedings. No public recognition was accorded to the provisional government by the United States Minister until after the Queen's abdication and when they were in effective possession of the Government buildings, the archives, the treasury, the barracks, the police station, and all the potential machinery of the Government." But a protest also accompanied said treaty, signed by the Queen and her ministers at the time she made way for the provisional government, which explicitly stated that she yielded to the superior force of the United States, whose Minister had caused United States troops to be landed at Honolulu and declared that he would support such provisional government. . . .

Name ______________________

Date ______________________

I conceived it to be my duty therefore to withdraw the treaty from the Senate for examination, and meanwhile to cause an accurate, full, and impartial investigation to be made of the facts attending the subversion of thc constitutional Government of Hawaii and the installment in its place of the provisional government. . . .

The report . . . justifies in my opinion the statement that when the President was led to submit the treaty to the Senate with the declaration that "the overthrow of the monarchy was not in any way promoted by this Government," and when the Senate was induced to receive and discuss it on that basis, both President and Senate were misled. . . .

The lawful Government of Hawaii was overthrown without the drawing of a sword or the firing of a shot by a process every step of which, it may be safely asserted, is directly traceable to and dependent for its success upon the agency of the United States acting through its diplomatic and naval representatives. . . .

By an act of war, committed with the participation of a diplomatic representative of the United States and without authority of Congress, the Government of a feeble but friendly and confiding people has been overthrown. A substantial wrong has thus been done which a due regard for our national character as well as the rights of the injured people requires we should endeavor to repair. The provisional government has not assumed a republican or other constitutional form, but has remained a mere executive council or oligarchy, set up without the assent of the people. It has not sought to find a permanent basis of popular support and has given no evidence of an intention to do so. . . .

. . . She [the Queen] surrendered not to the provisional government, but to the United States. She surrendered not absolutely and permanently, but temporarily and conditionally until such time as the facts could be considered by the United States. . . .

. . . I instructed Minister Willis to advise the Queen and her supporters of my desire to aid in the restoration of the status existing before the lawless landing of the United States forces at Honolulu on the 16th of January last. . . . The conditions suggested . . . contemplate a general amnesty to those concerned in setting up the provisional government and a recognition of all its bona fide acts and obligations. In short, they require that the past should be buried, and that the restored Government should reassume its authority as it its continuity had not been interrupted. These conditions have not proved acceptable to the Queen, and though she has been informed that they will be insisted upon, and that, unless acceded to, the efforts of the President to aid in the restoration of her Government will cease, I have not thus far learned that she is willing to yield them her acquiescence. . . .

In commending this subject to the extended powers and wide discretion of the Congress, I desire to add the assurance that I shall be much gratified to cooperate in any legislative plan which may be devised for the solution of the problem before us which is consistent with American honor, integrity, and morality.

1. Why was annexation such a serious problem?

Name ________________________

Date ________________________

2. What did Grover Cleveland's investigation reveal?

3. How did Cleveland regard the actions of the provisional government?

4. What did Cleveland propose to do?

5. How did Lili'uokalani react to Cleveland's proposal?

Part B.

On September 9, 1897, the Senate of the Republic of Hawaii passed a resolution consenting to the annexation of Hawaii. Attempts by the Congress of the United States to pass a treaty of annexation had failed. However, advocates of the annexation, including President William McKinley, were able to negotiate the passage of a joint resolution of the U.S. Congress formally approving the takeover of the islands by the United States on July 7, 1898. The excerpts in the document below are from the resolution passed by the Hawaiian Senate. Read the selection and answer the question that follows. Be prepared for class discussion.

Consent to the Annexation of Hawaii

Article I. The Republic of Hawaii hereby cedes absolutely and without reserve to the United States of America all rights of sovereignty of whatsoever kind in and over the Hawaiian Islands and their dependencies: and it is agreed that all the territory of and appertaining to the Republic of Hawaii is hereby annexed to the United States of America under the name of the Territory of Hawaii.

Article II. The Republic of Hawaii also cedes and hereby transfers to the United States the absolute fee and ownership of all public, government or crown lands, public buildings or edifices, ports, harbors, military equipment, and all other public property of every kind and description belonging to the government of the Hawaiian Islands, together with every right and appurtenance thereunto appertaining.

The existing laws of the United States relative to public lands shall not apply to such lands in the Hawaiian Islands: but the Congress of the United States shall enact special laws for their management and disposition. Provided: that all revenue from or proceeds of the same, except as regards such part thereof as may be used or occupied for the civil, military or naval purposes of the United States, or may be assigned for the use of the local government, shall be used solely for the benefit of the inhabitants of the Hawaiian islands for educational and other public purposes.

Name ____________________

Date ____________________

Article III. . . . The existing treaties of the Hawaiian Islands with foreign nations shall forthwith cease and determine, being replaced by such treaties as may exist, or as may be hereafter concluded between the United States and such foreign nations. The municipal legislation of the Hawaiian Islands, not enacted for the fulfillment of the treaty so extinguished, and not inconsistent with this treaty, not contrary to the Constitution of the United States, nor to any existing treaty of the United States, shall remain in force until the Congress of the United States shall otherwise determine.

Until legislation shall be exacted extending the United States Customs laws and regulations to the Hawaiian Islands, the existing Customs relations of the Hawaiian islands with the United States and other countries shall remain unchanged.

Article IV. The public debt of the Republic of Hawaii . . . is hereby assumed by the Government of the United States: but the liability of the United States in this regard shall in no case exceed $4,000,000. . . .

Article V. There shall be no further immigration of Chinese into the Hawaiian Islands, except upon such conditions as are now or may hereafter be allowed by the laws of the United States, and no Chinese by reason of anything herein contained shall be allowed to enter the United States from the Hawaiian Islands.

What eight points did the resolution propose?

Part C.

In June 1897, the deposed queen of Hawaii, Lili'uokalani, appeared in Washington, D.C. to protest formally the ratification of a proposed treaty that would make her island homeland a possession of the United States. Her regal demeanor and eloquent protest affected the ability of the pro-annexation supporters to obtain enough votes for the passage of the treaty and forced them to resort to the passage of a joint resolution to legitimize the American seizure of Hawaii. Below is her protest, in which she presents her argument against annexation. Read the selection and answer the questions that follow. Be prepared for class discussion.

Official Protest to the Treaty of Annexation

I, Lili'uokalani of Hawaii, by the will of God named heir apparent on the tenth day of April, A.D. 1877, and by the grace of God Queen of the Hawaiian Islands on the seventeenth day of January, A.D. 1893, do hereby protest against the ratification of a certain treaty, which, so I am informed, has been signed at Washington by Messrs. Hatch, Thurston, and Kinney, purporting to cede those Islands to the territory and dominion of the United States. I declare such a treaty to be an act of wrong toward the native and part-native people of Hawaii, an invasion of the rights

Name ________________________

Date ________________________

of the ruling chiefs, in violation of international rights both toward my people and toward friendly nations with whom they have made treaties, the perpetuation of the fraud whereby the constitutional government was overthrown, and, finally, an act of gross injustice to me.

Because the official protests made by me on the seventeenth day of January, 1893, to the so-called Provisional Government was signed by me, and received by said government with the assurance that the case was referred to the United States of America for arbitration.

Because that protest and my communications to the United States Government immediately thereafter expressly declare that I yielded my authority to the forces of the United States in order to avoid bloodshed, and because I recognized the futility of a conflict with so formidable a power.

Because the President of the United States [Grover Cleveland], the Secretary of State, and an envoy commissioned by them reported in official documents that my government was unlawfully coerced by the forces, diplomatic and naval, of the United States; that I was at the date of their investigations the constitutional ruler of my people.

Because neither the above-named commissioner nor the government which sends it has ever received any such authority from the registered voters of Hawaii, but derives its assumed powers from the so-called committee of public safety, organized on or about the seventeenth day of January, 1893, said committee being composed largely of persons claiming American citizenship, and not one single Hawaiian was a member thereof, or in any way participated in the demonstration leading to its existence.

Because my people about forty thousand in number, have in no way been consulted by those, three thousand in number, who claim the right to destroy the independence of Hawaii. My people constitute four-fifths of the legally qualified voters of Hawaii, and excluding those imported for the demands of labor, about the same proportion of the inhabitants.

Because said treaty ignores, not only the civic rights of my people, but, further, the hereditary property of their chiefs. Of the 4,000,000 acres composing the territory said treaty offers to annex, 1,000,000 or 915,000 acres has in no way been heretofore recognized as other than the private property of the constitutional monarch, subject to a control in no way differing from other items of a private estate.

Because it is proposed by said treaty to confiscate said property, technically called the crown lands, those legally entitled thereto, either now or in succession, receiving no consideration whatever for estates, their title to which has been always undisputed, and which is legitimately in my name at this date.

Because said treaty ignores, not only all professions of perpetual amity and good faith made by the United States in former treaties with the sovereigns representing the Hawaiian people, but all treaties made by those sovereigns with other friendly powers, and it is thereby in violation of international law.

Because, by treating with the parties claiming at this time the right to cede said territory of Hawaii, the Government of the United States receives such territory from the hands of those whom its own magistrates (legally elected by the people of the United States, and in office in 1893) pronounced fraudulently in power and unconstitutionally ruling Hawaii.

Name ______________________

Date ______________________

Therefore, I, Lili'uokalani of Hawaii, do hereby call upon the President of that nation, to whom alone I yielded my property and my authority, to withdraw said treaty (ceding said Islands) from further consideration. I ask the honorable Senate of the United States to decline to ratify said treaty, and I implore the people of this great and good nation, from whom my ancestors learned the Christian religion, to sustain their representatives in such acts of justice and equity as may be in accord with the principles of their fathers, and to the Almighty Ruler of the universe, to him who judgeth righteously, I commit my cause.

Done at Washington, District of Columbia, United States of America, this seventeenth day of June, in the year eighteen hundred and ninety-seven.

Lili'uokalani

Joseph Heleluhe
Wokeki Heleluhe } Witnesses
Julius A. Palmer

1. What did Lili'uokalani declare the treaty to be?

2. Why did Lili'uokalani surrender her government to the committee?

3. What did she say about the validity of the treaty?

4. How did the treaty ignore the hereditary rights of the monarchy and the Hawaiian chiefs?

5. To whom was Lili'uokalani referring to as the "magistrate" of the United States?

6. To whom did Lili'uokalani appeal for justice?

John Wesley Hardin and the Texas Rangers

Objectives

- To become familiar with the importance of the Texas Rangers and the maintenance of peace and order along the frontier
- To examine the differences between the legal rights of criminals in the nineteenth and twentieth centuries

Notes to the Teacher

The use of rangers as peacekeepers and law enforcement officers along America's frontier dates to colonial times. When southern frontiersmen from Tennessee, Mississippi, Alabama, and Louisiana moved into Texas at the beginning of the nineteenth century, they brought this concept with them. Originally organized under Mexican law in 1822, the Rangers were intended as a defense against Indian raids. Beginning in the early eighteenth century, the Kiowa and Comanche of the Staked Plains had formed a military alliance which would last until the Red River War (1874–1875). Both groups were raiding people who engaged in unending warfare. Prestige was determined by the skill of a warrior, and by the early nineteenth century, an annual spring raiding season had been established in order to reinforce this idea.

The first official Ranger companies were established in the spring of 1835 and consisted of sixty-five men and officers. Divided into three companies, they were directly answerable to the commander in chief of the Mexican army but were in reality an independent unit over which the Mexicans had little or no control. Paid the equivalent of $1.25 a day, they were expected to supply their own horses, equipment, and ammunition. The Rangers acted in a manner that was similar to the Minutemen in colonial times. They were to be ready at a moment's notice.

After a series of successful engagements against the Kiowa and Comanche, the government of the newly formed Republic of Texas recognized the efficiency and effectiveness of the Rangers in the protection of the frontier and the Rangers were continued by the new nation. Captain John Coffee Hays recruited and trained a group of men who were skilled in frontier warfare. During the Mexican War, the Rangers acted as the eyes and ears of General Zachary Taylor's army. Armed to the teeth, the Rangers were a ruthless and lethal force referred to by the Mexican guerrillas they fought as "los diablos Tejanos," the Texas Devils. Between the end of the Mexican War and 1874, the Rangers had no official function, although they did participate in the Red River War against the Comanches in 1874–75. The Civil War saw the Rangers at their least effective. Most able-bodied Rangers enlisted in the Confederate Army, and old men, boys, and rejects from the military life were the guardians of the Texas frontier.

In 1874, the Rangers were reconstituted by the Texas legislature, and two groups were established. Bandits and Native Americans were attacking the frontier in west Texas and along the Rio Grande. The Special Force, under the command of Captain Leander McNelly, was charged with maintaining the peace along the Rio Grande. By 1875, McNelly and his Rangers had brought peace and order along the Rio Grande. By killing one dozen desperados for every Ranger killed and publicly displaying the bodies, McNelly illustrated the fate of anyone who challenged the authority of the Rangers. During the Las Cuevas War, McNelly and his men violated the Mexican-U.S. border in pursuit of cattle thieves. The cattle thieves were captured, the cattle returned, and no one challenged the authority of the Rangers. The Frontier Battalion, under the leadership of Major John B. Jones, was dispatched to the rough lands of the western reaches of Texas to destroy the power of the Comanches and Kiowas who continued to raid settlements and to neutralize over three thousand desperados who had moved into central and west Texas during and after the Civil War. Members of the Frontier Battalion brought many Texas desperados to justice. One of the most infamous men captured by the Rangers was John Wesley Hardin. Hardin was captured when a Ranger named J. B. Armstrong ignored state boundaries and crossed Louisiana and Alabama in pursuit.

In this lesson, students examine the role played by the Rangers in maintaining peace along the frontier. Students examine documents connected to the capture of John Wesley Hardin. After comparing the method of Hardin's capture with modern legal restraints regarding extradition, students write a letter to the editor of the Comanche County, Texas, newspaper either in support of or against the method of Hardin's capture. Students should be familiar with the following Supreme Court cases before beginning the lesson: *Miranda v. Arizona* and *Gideon v. Wainwright.*

Reminder to Teachers

- Decide if the appropriate primary sources analysis worksheets from the appendix will be used in this lesson.
- Assign those sections of the basal textbook that are relevant to this lesson.

Procedure

1. Ask students to define *extradition* (*to remove an alleged criminal from one jurisdiction to another*). Explain that they are going to examine a case of extradition involving the Texas Rangers and John Wesley Hardin, a notorious outlaw. Distribute **Handout 11**, and have students read it and complete the questions for discussion. Review students' responses.

   Suggested Responses:

   1. *the alleged murder of Deputy Sheriff Charles Webb*
   2. *Hardin and his gang had been robbing trains in Alabama, Louisiana, and Texas.*
   3. *Armstrong was waiting for legal papers that could allow him to return Hardin to Texas.*
   4. *to prevent the people of Comanche from lynching him*
   5. *Hardin wasn't a "common" criminal, and his sentence reflected that.*
   6. *Hardin served most of his prison term, vowed to go straight, became a lawyer, eventually returned to his life of crime, and was shot to death in El Paso in 1895.*

   Ask students to define *writ of habeas corpus* (*a legal document that forces an individual to appear before a court, usually to answer for an alleged crime*). Discuss the main points of *Miranda v. Arizona* and *Gideon v. Wainwright.* (*They guarantee criminals the right to counsel, the right to remain silent, and the right to be warned that they can withhold information which might be self-incriminating.*) Ask students if Hardin's extradition could have taken place in the same manner today (*no*). Why? (*Alleged criminals today are protected by the Supreme Court's interpretation of the Bill of Rights.*)

2. Distribute **Handout 12**, and have students read it and complete the questions for discussion. Review students' responses.

   Suggested Responses:

   1. *Hardin has friends in town, and Armstrong worries they may try to rescue Hardin.*
   2. *He is waiting for a writ of habeas corpus, and he wants it sent by a courier.*

3. Distribute **Handout 13**, and have students read it and complete the questions for discussion. Review students' responses.

   Suggested Responses:

   Part A.

   1. *The Sheriff of Comanche County, whose deputy allegedly had been killed by Hardin, felt there was a threat of mob violence.*
   2. *Gillett was a young man who had previously earned a living by selling fish and game on the streets of Austin, the Texas state capital. This was a very important assignment, escorting the most important criminal in Texas.*

   Part B.

   1. *decorus and communicative, sleeps easily*
   2. *It took five days, with Hardin in iron.*
   3. *doesn't really say*
   4. *maybe the irons on his hands and feet, or the threat of being shot*

4. Conclude the lesson by instructing students to write a letter protesting or supporting the manner in which John Wesley Hardin was brought to justice. Have selected students read their letters.

Extension Activities

1. Have students investigate and report on the way in which frontier justice was administered in the cattle towns of Kansas or in Tombstone, Arizona, during the 1870s and 1880s.

2. Have students expand their research on the Texas Rangers. Instruct students to research the administration of justice in New York City during the later half of the nineteenth century and compare and contrast it with the justice of the frontier.

3. Have students view the film version of Larry McMurtry's novel *Deadman's Walk*, which portrays the Texas Rangers just after the Mexican War. Available on video, *Deadman's Walk* is reasonably accurate. The characters in the story and its sequel *Comanche Moon* reappear in McMurtry's classic *Lonesome Dove.*

Name ________________________

Date ________________________

"A Champion Desperado"

Read the resource sheet below, and be prepared to answer the questions that follow.

During the 1870s, Texas was home to a variety of murderous lawbreakers; however, none was so famous as John Wesley Hardin. Hardin was not a thief, nor was he a bandit. He was a murderer. It was said that during his life, he killed between twenty-five and thirty men, not counting Native Americans, Mexicans, or African Americans. In May 1874, Hardin was twenty-four years old, stood five feet nine inches in height, had blue eyes, and a murderous intent. He murdered a deputy sheriff named Charles Webb, of Comanche County, Texas. It was this action that caused the Texas Rangers to hunt Hardin down, with no respect to state boundaries. A four-thousand-dollar reward offered jointly by Texas and Louisiana resulted in thousands of would-be detectives setting out to capture him. The Adjutant General of Texas, William Steele, appointed Ranger John B. Armstrong to work on the Hardin case. A detective named John Duncan, from the adjutant's office, was assigned to work with Armstrong.

Hardin had begun to roam Texas and Louisiana at will, using numerous aliases and gathering a gang together. They proceeded to attack and harass railroad lines crisscrossing the states. With the cooperation of the railroads, Armstrong and Duncan found out that Hardin was headed to Pensacola, Florida. Gaining the cooperation of local lawmen, who no doubt would have preferred to have Hardin captured before he could wreak havoc in their town, Armstrong and Duncan planned to attempt to capture Hardin while he was still aboard the train.

Armstrong was to enter the train car facing Hardin, while Duncan and the Florida lawmen were to enter from the rear. For whatever reason, Duncan and the Florida lawmen failed to help Armstrong, who was left to confront Hardin alone. After being shot at by a member of Hardin's gang, Armstrong returned fire, killed the gang member, and was able to get close enough to pistol-whip Hardin and render him unconscious for two hours. The remaining members of the gang surrendered their weapons. Armstrong then ordered the train to leave the Pensacola station and proceed west out of town. At regular intervals along the tracks, Armstrong ordered the train stopped and the remaining members of Hardin's gang were dropped off one at a time along the tracks. When the train finally reached Whitney, Alabama, Hardin's hometown, Hardin was the only outlaw remaining in Armstrong's custody. Armstrong crossed Alabama by train, stopping off in Montgomery, where he awaited papers that would allow him to remove Hardin legally to Texas. When the papers finally arrived, Armstrong and his prisoner proceeded to the state capital at Austin, where Hardin was jailed. In the last week of September, Hardin was tried in Comanche, Texas, for the murder of Deputy Charles Webb. Rangers guarded him day and night while he was confined in Comanche's jail, partly to insure that none of Hardin's gang attempted to break him out of jail, and partly to insure that Charles Webb's friends didn't seize and lynch Hardin. Hardin was convicted of second-degree murder and sentenced to twenty-five years in the Texas State Prison at Huntsville. He was said to have wept at the verdict and declared that the jury was too hard on him but later declared the verdict to be fair because the jury was trying John Wesley Hardin, not a common criminal. On October 5, Ranger N. O. Reynolds delivered Hardin to the prison in Huntsville, where he proved to be a model prisoner. In 1893, Hardin was granted a pardon by Texas Governor Hogg. Hardin studied the law while in prison, and after his release, he was admitted to the bar, vowing to go

Name ______________________

Date ______________________

straight. His good intentions lasted for one year, and he returned to his life of crime. John Selman killed Hardin in El Paso, Texas in 1895.[1]

1. What action caused the Texas Rangers to hunt Hardin down?

2. Why did the railroads aid in the capture of Hardin?

3. Why did Armstrong stop in Montgomery?

4. Why were the Rangers guarding Hardin?

5. Why did Hardin feel the verdict of the jury was fair?

6. What happened to Hardin?

[1]Additional information about this topic can be found in *The Texas Rangers: A Century of Frontier Defense*, Walter Prescott Webb (Austin, Tex.: The University of Texas Press, 1965).

Name ________________________

Date ________________________

In Hot Pursuit

En route to Texas, Ranger John B. Armstrong proceeded to send the following series of telegrams to Adjutant General William Steele, informing him of the progress of his return to Texas. They are the only documented records of John Wesley Hardin's capture. Read the telegrams, and answer the questions that follow.

Whitney, Alabama
August 23, 1877

To General Wm. Steele

Arrested John Wesley Hardin, Pensacola, Florida, this P.M. He had four men with him. Had some lively shooting. One of their number killed, all the rest captured. Hardin fought desperately, closed in and took him by main strength. Hurried ahead the train then leaving for this place. We are waiting for a train to get away on. This is Hardin's home and his friends are trying to rally men to release him. Have some good citizens with [me] and will make it interesting.

J. B. Armstrong
Lt. State Troops

Montgomery, Alabama
August 24, 1877

To General Wm. Steele

Arrived this A.M. Prisoner in jail. No papers whatever received by governor. What is the matter? [Armstrong has requested a writ of habeas corpus, which will allow him to take Hardin across state lines and return him to Texas.]

J. B. Armstrong
Lt. Spl. State Troops

Montgomery, Alabama
August 24, 1877

To General Wm. Steele

Hardin taken out on writ of habeas corpus. Case continued to Wednesday. Send another requisition by man or express. Am afraid it will miscarry by mail as did the first. Answer.

J. B. Armstrong

To Adj. General Wm. Steele

It is all day now. On our way. Papers O.K.

J. B. Armstrong[2]

1. Why is Armstrong anxious to get out of town with his prisoner?

2. What is Ranger Armstrong waiting for, and how does he want it sent?

[2]Telegrams from Ranger John B. Armstrong to General William Steele, Papers of the Texas Adjutant General's Office, in *The Texas Rangers*, Webb, 300–301.

Name ______________________

Date ______________________

Guarding the Desperado

Part A.

The Rangers protected Hardin before and during his trial and transferred him after his conviction to the Texas state prison at Huntsville. Below is a short account of these events as they appeared in the memoirs of James B. Gillett, who served with the Rangers between 1875 and 1881. Gillett was eighteen years old when he was sent to escort Hardin from Austin to the Comanche County jail. Read the following selections and complete the questions for discussion.

> In the summer of 1877 Lieutenant Armstrong of Captain Hall's company, assisted by Detective Jack Duncan of Dallas, Texas, captured the notorious John Wesley Hardin. It has been said by some wag [a witty person] that Texas, the largest state in the Union, has never produced a real world's champion at anything. Surely this critic overlooked Hardin, the champion desperado of the world. His life is too well known in Texas for me to go into detail, but, according to his own story, which I have before me, he killed no fewer than twenty-seven men, the last being Charley Webb, deputy sheriff of Brown County, Texas. So notorious had Hardin become that the state of Texas offered $4,000 reward for his capture. Hardin had left Texas and at the time of his capture was in Florida. His captors arrested and overpowered him while he was sitting in a passenger coach.
>
> In September, 1877, Sheriff Wilson of Comanche County, in whose jurisdiction Hardin had killed Webb, came to Austin to convey the prisoner to Comanche for trial. Wilson requested the governor for an escort of rangers. Lieutenant Reynolds' company, being in Austin at the time, was ordered to accompany Wilson and protect Hardin from mob violence. [A lynch mob from Brown County attacked and lynched the brother-in-law of Hardin and two friends when they refused to tell where Hardin was hiding.] . . .
>
> The day we left Austin between one and two thousand people gathered about the Travis County jail to see this notorious desperado. . . . Heavily shackled and handcuffed, the prisoner walked very slowly between us [Gillett and Henry Thomas]. The boy who had sold fish and game on the streets of Austin [Gillett] was now guarding the most desperate criminal in Texas; it was glory enough for me.[3]

1. Why was it necessary to protect Hardin?

2. Why do you think this was an important event in the life of James B. Gillett?

[3]James B. Gillett, *Six Years with the Texas Rangers: 1875–1881*, ed. M. M. Quaife (Lincoln, Nebr.: University of Nebraska Press, 1925), 85–86.

Name ________________________

Date ________________________

A Ranger's Opinion

One of the Rangers who guarded Hardin during his stay in the Comanche jail prepared the following account of the scene before Hardin's trial. The account appeared, anonymously at the time, in the *Galveston News*. Read it, and answer the discussion questions.

Comanche City, September 29, 1877

Editors News:

Day before yesterday Lieut. Reynolds, commanding Co. E. of the Frontier Battalion, arrived at this place guarding John Wesley Hardin. The Rangers were five days on the road with their prisoner. Hardin deported himself with the utmost decorum, evincing no restlessness, though his patience was sorely tried by the gaping crowds who gathered at the noon and evening camps to stare him in the face with a curiosity that knew no sense of delicacy. He was quite communicative, talking freely of his terrible adventures, expressing regrets for what he termed his errors, and hopes for the future. He is what the ladies would call a blonde; about five feet ten inches high; and is fairly educated in English and the common school branches. He has suffered with one old bullet wound on the trip hither. He is confined in the jail at this place, heavily sealed on the inside with oak, containing an iron cage. He is also ironed and guarded by Rangers, who remain within the prison walls both by day and night. A company of Rangers are camped in the back yard of the prison, so that the public may rest assured that there is no possibility of the prisoner's escape on the one hand or suffering by mob violence on the other. . . .

Your correspondent has heard many stories of John Wesley Hardin, and can not but believe that some of them were greatly exaggerated. Many have asserted that he is unable to sleep with any degree of comfort to himself or those within hearing of him; that, disturbed by appalling dreams, he is wont to spring, howling like a mad man, from his bed, to grapple with phantom foes or cower whimpering on the floor. One narrator tells of a St. Louis hotel clerk who goes limping on crutches from a pistol ball received by making too hasty a visit to the dreadful dreamer while a spasm, such as I have described, was on him. But I have guarded this wild man, the report of whose bloody crimes has caused so much shuddering, whose name was "bug bear" to the timid tourist in Texas. Yes, I have guarded him at midnight, when the moonlight was reflected in the dew drops on the prairie sedge, and in the tangled brush that skirts the cow-house. Alone and standing among the sleeping rangers I have gazed upon the face of him I guarded, John Wesley Hardin, the gentlest sleeper of them all. Sometimes a troubled look disturbed his countenance for an instant; once he murmured "Johnny," his little son's name, but in the main his sleep was calmer than the moonlit stream flowing past me to the sea. If any demons ever haunted his bedchamber, they kept aloof from his bivouac. Were the irons on his limbs the potent charms that awed them away, or was it the cold blue gleam of the sentinel's Winchester [rifle]? Perhaps some spiritualists can answer.

Mervyn[4]

[4] *Galveston News*, 3 October 1877, in *The Texas Rangers*, Webb, 302–3.

Name ______________________

Date ______________________

1. How did Mervyn characterize Hardin?

2. Describe Hardin's trip from Austin to Comanche.

3. Why did Mervyn believe the stories about Hardin were greatly exaggerated?

4. What reasons did Mervyn give for Hardin's model behavior?

To Win Unfading Glory: African Americans in the Spanish-American War

Objectives

- To discuss the attitude of African Americans towards service in the Spanish-American War and their place in society
- To examine the role played by African-American soldiers during the Spanish-American War

Notes to the Teacher

From our very beginnings, African Americans have served in the defense of our nation. From those who fought in the American Revolution to those who gave their lives in Vietnam, African Americans have served proudly and with distinction. In 1863, during America's Civil War, the United States Colored Troops were organized. These volunteer companies included such famed units as the Fifty-fourth Massachusetts. When the war ended, thousands of USCT troopers were mustered out of the service.

After the war, the Army was reorganized, and the Army Organization Act was passed in 1866. This act created four additional cavalry units including the Ninth and Tenth Cavalry, which were to be composed of "colored" troopers and white officers. African-American infantry units such as the Twenty-fourth Infantry were also established. These men came from a range of backgrounds. Some were educated; others were former slaves. Most of the men who served in the Ninth Cavalry came from Florida, Louisiana, and Texas. They fought primarily against the Indians of the Southwest and patrolled the border between the United States and Mexico, protecting settlers and the government mail. The Tenth Cavalry was organized in St. Louis, Missouri, and was initially based at Fort Leavenworth, Kansas. They fought extended campaigns against the Cheyennes, Kiowas, Comanches, and Apaches in Kansas, New Mexico, Arizona, and the Indian Territory (Oklahoma). During the campaign against the Comanches in 1871, the Tenth came to be known as the Buffalo Soldiers, a name bestowed on them by the Native Americans, who respected the tireless marching and trail skills of the soldiers. To the Native Americans, the soldiers were synonymous with the rugged and revered buffalo.

African-American troopers fought with bravery and honor under Teddy Roosevelt at San Juan Hill, patrolled the U.S. border with Mexico, and served as part of the punitive force led by John J. Pershing into Mexico, in pursuit of the legendary bandit Pancho Villa.

In this lesson, students examine the role played by African Americans in the Spanish-American War and the attitude of the African-American population toward participation in the war. Students read and discuss four documents: an excerpt from a sermon delivered by the Reverend H. H. Proctor before the Colored Militia of Atlanta, Georgia, urging them to participate in the war; two excerpts from accounts of the Twenty-fourth Infantry's and Tenth Cavalry's participation in the war; and a letter of commendation written by General Joseph Wheeler, the commanding officer of the African-American troopers serving in Cuba. To conclude the lesson, students write a letter to a newspaper in which they commend the efforts of African-American troopers.

Reminder to Teachers

- Decide if the appropriate primary sources analysis worksheets from the appendix will be used in this lesson.
- Assign those sections of the basal textbook that are relevant to this lesson.

Procedure

1. Ask students to volunteer information they might have about the service of African Americans in our armed forces. They might cite *Glory* (service in the Civil War), service on the Plains, during Korea, Vietnam, in the Persian Gulf, and the Tuskegee airmen. Explain that most African Americans who served before Vietnam would have served in the ranks. Very few African

Americans were officers. Mention Henry C. Flipper, an African-American graduate of West Point, who served with Pershing in the Southwest, and General Benjamin O. Davis, Sr., who served with distinction in World War II and Korea.

2. Review and discuss briefly the status of African Americans in the United States during the period of Reconstruction and the racial climate of the times. Divide the class into small groups of three or four and distribute **Handout 14.** Divide the handout into three or four parts, and have each group read and analyze a section. Allow students fifteen minutes to complete this analysis. Discuss Reverend Proctor's sermon using the following questions:

   - Why was Reverend Proctor led to question the attitude of African Americans toward participation in the war?

     (*present action will have an influence on the destiny of future African Americans as a part of the American nation; conflict of opinion regarding duty and this war*)

   - What arguments did Reverend Proctor say had been given as reasons against African American participation in the war?

     (*It was a white man's war; let the whites fight it out. African Americans had been treated badly in the years following the Civil War. African Americans had fought bravely for their country in the Civil War and against the Indians, and they were not treated any better or differently by people.*)

   - What were Reverend Proctor's reasons for African Americans to fight in the war?

     (*African Americans should be loyal to the United States and exhibit patriotism; this was their first opportunity to fight as freemen; the shedding of their blood in defense of the nation would greatly reinforce their claims to American citizenship; this was a righteous war being fought for a larger liberty; it was an opportunity to remove prejudice; it presented an opportunity to become part of the nation, not continue to be a nation within a nation; it was an opportunity to remove barriers between North and South and black and white.*)

   Ask students if they would have agreed with Reverend Proctor and signed up to fight.

3. With students still in their groups, distribute copies of **Handouts 15** and **16** so that approximately one half of the class has **Handout 15** and the other half **Handout 16.** Ask each group to read the handout and cite examples of action on the part of the members of the Twenty-fourth Infantry or the Tenth Cavalry that illustrate the bravery of African-American troopers who served in the Spanish-American War. Ask each group to share one example with the class.

4. Distribute **Handout 17**, and ask a student to read the letter aloud. Ask if students believe the letter would have been common during the time, given the racial climate of the period.

5. Direct students to assume the role of a member of the American forces serving in Cuba during the Spanish-American War. Have them write a letter to their hometown newspaper describing the bravery and service of African-American troopers in the war. Have selected students share their letters with the class.

Extension Activities

1. Have students research and report on the service of African-American troopers during the Indian Wars.

2. Have students research and report on the participation of Henry O. Flipper in the punitive expedition against Pancho Villa in 1917. Flipper syndicated his journal and it appeared in many African-American newspapers at the time. This might be a good source for students to examine.

Name ____________________

Date ____________________

A Sermon on the War

The following excerpt is from a sermon preached by Reverend H. H. Proctor at the First Congregational Church of Atlanta, Georgia, on May 1, 1898, before the assembled Colored Military Companies of Atlanta. Read and analyze your assigned section of the excerpt, and be prepared for discussion.

Not for reasons of greed or vengeance do we justify this war. . . . The state of things that exists in Cuba is terrible. The island is laid waste, homes are desolate, the people are starving, multitudes are dying. And this almost in sight of our shores. . . . This destruction is intolerable and in the spirit of Christ they [the American people] rise up in just indignation and declare their compassion for the multitudes of Cuba. . . .

But the main point I wish to bring before you tonight is what attitude should colored citizens sustain toward the government in this crisis? I am led to do this from two considerations. The first is the future bearing our present action will have upon our destiny as a people in this country; and the second is the conflict of opinion that prevails in regard to our duty in this war. . . .

It is said that this is a white man's war, and, therefore, let the white fight it out. . . . If you say this is a white man's war, then you are bound to accept the doctrine that this is a white man's country. If this is a white man's country then the black man has no place in it, and consequently no rights that a white man is bound to respect. This is God's country, and it belongs to the people in it, be they black or white, red or yellow.

It is said that we are wrongly treated and therefore should sulk in our tents. I admit that we are wronged. God knows that. Call over the catalogue of wrongs and which of them are we not heir to? But in my mind this constitutes a reason why we should be loyal. If in this critical hour we should be disloyal, would that not serve as a justification in the eyes of our enemies for all the wrongs inflicted upon us? . . .

It is said we have fought for this country, and it treats us no better now let the white man fight it out themselves. It is true we have fought in every war; but has the motive of our action been beyond cavil? Is it not said that we fought in 1776 with the hope of freedom? In 1812 under the inspiration of the lash? In 1863 under the impulse of emancipation? do we not grant the imputations; but have we not opportunity now to exhibit a patriotism unselfish beyond dispute? For the first time in our American experience we should fight, not as slaves, not as freed men, but as freemen.

Then, I do not grant that we have not been helped by our participation in the wars of the past. The blood we have shed in our national wars has done much to enforce our claim to American citizenship. Our part in these wars has put argument in the mouths of our friends, and public sentiment has been turned in our favor. . . .

I pass on to some positive considerations. Why should we be loyal in this crisis? I do not, however, take stock in some of the reasons advanced.

We do not need to fight at this time to show that we are brave; that has been demonstrated. That monument on Boston common erected in honor of the first martyrs in the Revolutionary War, the noble words of Andrew Jackson to the colored men who formed the breastworks at New Orleans, the record of the two hundred thousand black soldiers in the civil war—these tell the world of the black man's bravery. You remember the incident at Fort Wagner. Colonel Shaw made a brilliant

Name ____________________

Date ____________________

charge against great odds. The color bearer fell, but another caught the flag and carried it to the top of the fort. Tho wounded as he stood before the rain of bullets he held to the flag until retreat, and when they brought Sergeant Carney to the hospital amid the cheers of his wounded comrades he said: "Boys, the old flag never touched the ground." Such men have established our claim to bravery.

We do not need to fight to show our loyalty. We have not only showed our loyalty in time of war, but at a time when it is more difficult to do so. I refer to times of peace. What portion of our complex citizenry today is more loyal than the black? At the belated call of their country they came two hundred thousand strong, and in the days of subsequent peace they showed the genuineness of their loyalty by settling down to hard work. If our loyalty has not been demonstrated in the past, we must despair of doing so now.

The real reason why the duty of the hour demands our loyalty is in this. Our country is engaged in a righteous war. It is a war for larger liberty. The freedom of manhood, the purity of womanhood, the future of childhood—these are in the womb of this struggle. It is an appeal to the highest sentiments. Our country is responding to the call. We are a real part of this country, and nothing that concerns her is without interest to us. We are not Afro-Americans, but Americans to the manor born. There should be no hyphen in American citizenship. . . .

We have an opportunity to remove prejudice. On every side we are hampered by prejudices. These prejudices have not been reasoned up, and they cannot be reasoned down. We must live them down, and we have never had a better opportunity than now. Before noble action, prejudice will vanish as the mist before the rising sun. If this war could produce an American Maceo the estimation in which the Negro is held would be heightened fifty per cent. If, when the history of this war is written and her epics sung, the Negro hero shall share in the glory, you will see a revolution in public sentiment.

We have an opportunity to fuse with the nation. Practically we are a nation within a nation. Like an island in a great sea the current of the nation's life sweeps around us. This nation has been greatly divided. Sectional and racial lines make serious divisions. . . . Perhaps Providence has brought us to this hour that He might fuse this nation in one. The North and the South so regard it for them. The sectional breach is closing. . . .

I regard it as a serious calamity should the fading of the color line not keep pace with that of the sectional line. I would that when cruel Spain is driven from the western world, when the American navy has cast anchor, when the volunteer soldier returns to private life, when fraternal relations are resumed between Washington and Madrid, and when the white-winged messenger of peace spans the seas, I would then that there should not only be no North and no South, but also no black and no white.

To this end I pray you let your loyalty be like the honor of Caesar's wife—above suspicion! If the nation's call comes to us let us go to the front and fight for the flag like men, and, God helping us, bring back the grand old flag with her honor unsullied and her glory undimmed.[1]

[1]Reverend H. H. Proctor, "The Duty of Colored Citizens to Their Country," 1 May 1898. Library of Congress, Rare Book and Special Collections Division, Daniel A. P. Murray Pamphlets Collection.

Name ________________________

Date ________________________

Under Fire with the Twenty-fourth Infantry in Cuba

The Twenty-fourth Infantry was composed of African-American soldiers and white officers. They, together with the Ninth and Tenth Cavalry, which were also African American, served with distinction during the Indian Wars in Arizona and New Mexico and in the Spanish-American War in Cuba. Besides serving as a fighting force in Cuba, the Infantry worked as nurses in yellow fever hospitals. Read the selection, and be prepared to describe the service of the Twenty-fourth Infantry in Cuba.

Early the next morning, long before sunrise, the enemy, irritated by their dreadful defeat of the night before, opened volley after volley upon our men, who now occupied the most important position along the whole line; but too late—the men had worked all night with improvised implements, using, in many cases, their muskets for shovels and their bayonets for spades, and had thus fortified themselves against the enemy's fire. All day long with nothing to eat or drink did these heroes lay in those narrow trenches, beneath the parching rays of a tropical sun. Every stitch of their clothes wringing wet from fording the river and from the dense dew for which Cuba is noted; lying on the bare ground with not a stitch to protect them or keep them warm; kept constantly on duty, while other regiments lurked about at the foot of the hill, and went to the rear where they could get abundant provisions—these men were yet cheerful through it all.

For fourteen long days did they endure almost unbearable hardships until almost demoralized by sickness, fatigue, and hunger, when, to the joy of every man the surrender was announced. Relieved greatly by this peaceful announcement they hoped soon for better fare; to be sent somewhere that they might rest and recover, but this was not to be. At 4 P.M. of the 14th of July, the day on which the surrender was announced, volunteers were called for to nurse the sick inmates of the rapidly increasing yellow fever hospital already established at Siboney. When eight regiments had been consulted and refused, the colored troops were called upon, and without a murmur they gladly accepted, marching from Santiago to Siboney, a distance of about fifteen miles, through almost complete darkness, passing through places so dense and dark that they were compelled to clasp hands in order to find their way. This was the worst night experienced while in Cuba.

Arriving at Siboney about 4 A.M. of July 16th they lay down with clothes soaked in perspiration on the ground that was daily drenched by rains. The next day nurses were called for, and almost all volunteered. However, only eighty-four were chosen, but within two weeks eighty more were called upon to fill the places made vacant by sickness and death—for only four of the first relay remained for duty.

Their fare was better here, but the awful scourge of the yellow fever soon thinned their ranks to a minimum. One month and ten days they remained at Siboney, nursing the sick, burying the dead, building tents, burning and disinfecting buildings, and performing every duty of camp life.[2]

[2]Herschel V. Cashin, et al., *Under Fire with the Tenth U.S. Cavalry* (1899; reprint, New York: Arno Press, 1969), 130–31.

Name ______________________

Date ______________________

Lieutenant Johnson's Daring Expedition

Below is an excerpt from an account of an expedition by the Tenth Cavalry to resupply Cuban army troops under the leadership of General Gomez. Read the excerpt, and be prepared to describe the service of the Tenth in Cuba.

> During the Spanish-American war, Troop M, Tenth Cavalry, left Port Tampa on the steamer Florida, June 20th, under the command of First Lieutenant Carter P. Johnson, of Troop H, Tenth United States Cavalry, with supplies for General Gomez's army. Besides ammunition, rations, and rifles there were five companies of Cuban soldiers on board under the command of General Nunez, who was accompanied by his staff. These Cubans called themselves American citizens. Our expedition consisted of three vessels—two transport and one gunboat. We were out thirteen days before we sighted land. The sea was perfectly smooth and the tropical heat very intense. We had to give special attention to the horses; for they were situated near the boiler room where the heat was so very great that it was almost unbearable. Our horses got along very well. Our losses were very small considering the condition of the weather.
>
> Our first combat with the Spanish was on the 30th of June, when we tried to effect a landing in the southeast corner of Santa Clara Province. We were told by the Cuban general on board of our transport that General Maximo Gomez would meet us at this point.
>
> On the 25th of July, the Cubans on board of our transports attempted to land, but were met by a volley of mauser bullets from the Spanish forces. At this point we had to fight, and General M. Gomez, who saw the effort we put forth, said that he had never witnessed greater bravery than was exhibited by our men. Troop M gained a reputation that each member should well be proud of. The commander-in-chief of the Cuban army, General Gonzellas, said of the troop when he was approached after the battle in regard to Negro generals: "If you will be as brave in the future to your country as you have proved yourself to-day it will not be very long before you will have generals in the army of the United States." Just after we had landed and marched to the place pointed out for our camp, we found dead bodies of Cubans and Spanish soldiers in every direction. We camped in a cocoanut grove. The land was in an awful condition. Buzzards were seen in every direction and if you wanted to locate a Cuban camp all you had to do would be look out for a large number of buzzards.
>
> In some of the camps, or forts taken by us from the Spanish forces we found an abundance of provision. A great number of cattle and chickens had been penned up for future use. The sights seen in the forts and on the battlefields were awful in their many grim aspects, and Troop M may never witness such sights again. Dead Cubans and Spaniards could be seen lying in an exposed condition, and the buzzards would feast upon them. At the mouth of the Rio de Sasa River we encountered the bitter opposition of the enemy, and thence on until our victory was won.
>
> Sergeant James B. Jelkas,
> Troop M[3]

[3]Cashin, *Under Fire with the Tenth U.S. Cavalry*, 175–76.

Name ______________________

Date ______________________

General Wheeler Commends His Troops

African-American soldiers served alongside white troopers during the Spanish-American War. Under the leadership of Major General Joseph Wheeler, a veteran of the Civil War, they fought with distinction. Below is a letter from General Wheeler to his men after their service at what was to come to be known as the Battle of San Juan Hill. Eighteen African Americans would be awarded the Congressional Medal of Honor, the highest military honor our nation can bestow, for service and bravery in the Indian Wars and in Cuba during the Spanish-American War. Read the excerpt, and be prepared for discussion.

Headquarters Cavalry Division, Camp Wikoff, L. I., September 20, 1898.

To the Officers and Soldiers, of the Cavalry Division, Army of Santiago:

The duties for which the troops comprising the cavalry division were brought together have been accomplished.

On June 14th we sailed from Tampa, Florida, to encounter in the sickly season the diseases of the tropical Island of Cuba, and to face and attack the historic legions of Spain in positions chosen by them and which for years they had been strengthening by every art and contrivance known to the skillful military engineers of Europe.

On the 23d one squadron each of the First and Tenth [African American] Regular Cavalry and two squadrons of the First Volunteer Cavalry [the Rough Riders], in all nine hundred and sixty-four officers and men landed on Cuban soil. These troops marched on foot fourteen miles, and, early on the morning of the 24th, attacked and defeated double their number of regular Spanish soldiers under the command of Lieutenant-General Linares. Eagerly and cheerfully you pushed onward, and on July 1st, the First, Third, Sixth, Ninth and Tenth Regular Cavalry and the First Volunteer Cavalry, forded the San Juan River and gallantly swept over San Juan Hill, driving the enemy from its crest. Without a moment's halt you formed, aligning the division upon the First Infantry division under General Kent, and, together with these troops, you bravely charged and carried the formidable intrenchments of Fort San Juan. The entire force which fought and won this great victory was less than seven thousand men.

The astonished enemy though still protected by the strong works to which he had made his retreat, was so stunned by your determined valor that his only thought was to devise the quickest means of saving himself from further battle. The great Spanish fleet hastily sought escape from the harbor and was destroyed by our matchless navy.

After seizing the fortifications of San Juan ridge, you, in the darkness of night, strongly intrenched the position your valor had won.

Reinforced by Bates' Brigade on your left and Lawton's Division on your right, you continued the combat until the Spanish army of Santiago Province succumbed to the superb prowess and courage of American arms. Peace promptly followed, and you return to receive the plaudits of seventy millions of people.

The valor displayed by you was not without sacrifice. Eighteen per cent., or nearly one in five, of the cavalry division fell on the field either killed or wounded. We mourn the loss of those heroic dead, and a grateful country will always revere their memory.

Name ______________________

Date ______________________

Whatever may be my fate, wherever my steps may lead, my heart will always burn with increasing admiration for your courage in action, your fortitude under privation and your constant devotion to duty in its highest sense, whether in battle, in bivouac, or upon the march.

(Signed) Joseph Wheeler,
Major-General U.S.V., Commanding.[4]

[4]Cashin, *Under Fire with the Tenth U.S. Calvalry*, 150–51.

Lesson 8—Politics

Charles Guiteau: Presidential Assassin

Objectives

- To examine the circumstances surrounding the assassination of James A. Garfield
- To discuss the passage of the Pendleton Civil Service Act of 1883 as a direct response to Garfield's assassination

Notes to the Teacher

History books often refer to Charles Guiteau, the assassin of President James A. Garfield, as a disgruntled office seeker. While it is true that Guiteau did seek a political appointment from James G. Blaine, Garfield's Secretary of State, he was also a deeply disturbed man who struggled most of his life with mental illness. After twenty years of failure, Guiteau seized upon the politics of the Republican Party in 1880. A conflict between the Stalwarts, led by Roscoe Conklin, and the Half-breeds, led by James G. Blaine, captured Guiteau's attention. Moving to Washington from New York, Guiteau harassed and annoyed the members of the White House staff with his continuous stream of letters addressed to Garfield and the members of his staff and administration. When he was thwarted in his attempt to meet with Blaine to explain his theories about how the government should operate, Guiteau took to the streets of Washington. He proclaimed his unhappiness with the current administration and demanded that the American people rise up and replace Garfield with a leader more responsive to the problems confronting America—Charles Guiteau. By mid-1881, Guiteau had decided that the only way to save America was to remove James A. Garfield from his position as President of the United States, through violent means if necessary. By mid-June he had sent letters to both James G. Blaine and William T. Sherman explaining his actions before they occurred. Both Blaine and Sherman claimed never to have seen the letters, and Guiteau was ignored.

On July 2, 1881, as Garfield waited for a train to take him to meet his family who were vacationing in Elburon, New Jersey, Guiteau shot Garfield twice—once in the arm and once in the back. Garfield was to die a slow and lingering death. His doctors probed and probed, often with dirty instruments, in an attempt to locate the bullet which had lodged in the president's back. Even inventor Alexander Graham Bell was called upon to examine the president, using a primitive form of metal detector. Infection caused Garfield's death in September 1881.

Guiteau was arrested and sent to the District of Columbia's jail, and after Garfield's death, he was charged with murder. A seven-month-long trial saw Guiteau convicted and sentenced to hang, even though he was delusional and could not participate in his defense. His family and his lawyers pleaded for mercy, but none was granted, and on July 30, 1892, Charles Guiteau was hanged in Washington, D.C.

During Guiteau's trial, newspaper coverage stressed the idea of assassination by a disgruntled office seeker, and Congress reacted with the passage of the Pendleton Act of 1883, which established the civil service system and began a regulation of political patronage. The Pendleton Act was largely ineffective in controlling political patronage. While it did establish the Civil Service Commission, the act regulated only ten percent of appointed jobs within the government. Fully ninety percent of government employees still remained in patronage jobs, with no controls over the process or criteria for selection.

In this lesson, students read and discuss short excerpts from a manifesto written by Guiteau explaining his actions to the American people and General William T. Sherman, confessing to the assassination of the president weeks before the event took place. Students also examine and discuss an account of Garfield's last moments before his death, the official bulletin issued by the White House at the time of Garfield's death, and analyze a memorial poem written to commemorate Garfield's death. To conclude, students become familiar with portions of the Pendleton Act of 1883, work in small groups to produce a more effective act to regulate government patronage, and share their work with the class.

Reminder to Teachers

- Decide if the appropriate primary sources analysis worksheets from the appendix will be used in this lesson.
- Assign those sections of the basal textbook that are relevant to this lesson.

Procedure

1. Ask if any students have relatives or friends who are employed by the national, state, or local governments. Ask students to define *civil service* (*civilian government workers who are appointed on merit rather than elected to serve in the government*). Ask for examples of the types of jobs (*postal workers, office workers, bureau of motor vehicles, police, and fire fighters*). Ask what the procedure is for obtaining employment (*taking a competitive test*). Ask students to define *political patronage* (*the power to give jobs or favors*). Explain that during the late nineteenth century, most government employees were appointed because they knew someone or were related to someone in the government, or because they had performed a favor, usually political in nature, for someone and were rewarded in turn by an elected or appointed official in a particular political party.

2. Ask students if they are familiar with Charles Guiteau. Most will probably be unfamiliar with him, and few will be able to identify him as a presidential assassin. Distribute **Handout 18,** and have students read it. Have them give some examples of Guiteau's unstable behavior prior to 1880 (*could not stay in one place for very long; had delusions about his employability; tried to extort money from the Oneida Community; allegedly attacked his sister with an ax; abusive toward wife*). Ask students if they believe that Garfield's assassination could have been prevented. Most students will answer yes. Ask how it could have been prevented. (*Attention could have been paid to the letters written by Guiteau and to his increasingly bizarre behavior.*)

3. Distribute **Handout 19**. Have students read it, and use the following questions for discussion:

   - How do these documents reflect Guiteau's state of mind?

     (*They don't make sense.*)

   - What was the general opinion of the public towards Guiteau?

     (*He was obviously imbalanced, but this had little bearing on the public view that Guiteau should be executed for his crime.*)

4. Distribute **Handout 20,** and have students read it while keeping in mind the following discussion questions:

   - How did the newspapers foster the image of Garfield as a martyred hero?

     (*somber and reverential tone; how the family bore the ordeal of grief*)

   - In the poem, what images invoke heroic qualities?

     (*prime of manhood, honor's dizziest height, eagle passing into the clouds and ascending heavenward, bravely strove, grief like a kinsman, bear home the soldier chief, beloved of his country*)

   Discuss the differences between modern use of media to raise dead celebrities to heroic stature. (Princess Diana and Kurt Cobain might be good examples.)

5. Distribute **Handout 21,** and have students read it. Ask students to define the principal points of the document.

   Suggested Responses:

   - *competitive testing to determine the appointment of the highest scoring employees in the Department of the Treasury and in the postal service*
   - *No person employed by the government shall be forced to make political contributions.*
   - *Those who had served honorably in the military would not lose any preference they might have for appointment.*
   - *Only two members of the same family may be employed by the government.*

- *No Senator, member of the House of Representatives, or member of the Executive branch may use their influence to obtain an appointment for any individual.*
- *No one may solicit political contributions on government property.*

Discuss whether the Pendleton Act of 1883 was an effective control of civil service employment. (*No, because only two departments, the Treasury and Post Office, less than ten percent of all federal employees, were affected by the act.*)

6. To conclude, divide students into small groups of four or five. Have students assume the role of members of Congress in 1883, and tell them to create a law controlling political patronage in the United States. Their act must include a paragraph explaining the purpose of the law, an explanatory paragraph listing the criteria required for government employment, and a concluding paragraph explaining how the law is to be administered. Have each group share its results for evaluation by the class.

Extension Activities

1. Arrange for a member of the local civil service administration to speak to the class about current regulations for employment.
2. Have students examine the role of other assassins of prominent Americans (such as Leon Czolgosz, Lee Harvey Oswald, and James Earl Ray), the motives for their actions, and the influence they have had on American history.

Name ______________________

Date ______________________

Charles Guiteau

Read the following information, and be prepared for discussion.

Born in Freeport, Illinois, on September 8, 1840, into a family whose patriarch was a stern and demanding man, Charles Guiteau seemed to be destined for a life of anonymity. When he indicated a desire to attend college, his father refused. Later, an inheritance from his maternal grandfather allowed Charles to attend college despite his father's wishes, and he enrolled at the University of Michigan. Unhappy, Guiteau turned to the teachings of nineteenth-century religious reformer John Humphrey Noyes, the founder of the Oneida Community. In 1865, five years after Guiteau joined the Oneida community, he informed the community's leaders that he had been chosen by God to spread the community's beliefs through the publication of a daily newspaper. He moved to Hoboken, New Jersey, where he published a struggling newspaper called the *Daily Theocrat.* By July 1865, Guiteau had left New Jersey and returned to the Oneida community in New York, where he remained until again departing the community in December 1865. Guiteau was offered a job in his brother-in-law George Scoville's law office in Chicago, where he worked only a few months before returning to New York. Guiteau informed everyone he would have a job writing editorials for Henry Ward Beecher's newspaper, *The Independent,* and was extremely disappointed to find that the only available jobs involved selling subscriptions and advertisements on commission.

Discouraged and having few prospects of success, Guiteau engaged in a scheme to force the Oneida community to repay him for work allegedly performed while living there. A series of threatening letters from Guiteau were regarded as extortion by the lawyers for the community, and he was warned to cease all communication with the community. In 1868, Guiteau returned to Chicago where he worked and studied in a law office, eventually passing the Illinois bar and setting up a small law office. Guiteau also entered into a marriage, which mirrored his unhappy life. He was abusive toward his wife, often locking her in a closet for days at a time. In 1874, she divorced him. By 1875, Guiteau's behavior had become bizarre. He moved again into his sister's home, where he reportedly threatened to attack her with an ax. Frightened by this behavior, his sister discussed institutionalizing him. Guiteau disappeared. Between 1874 and 1880, he became an itinerant preacher, after having been a regular attendee at Dwight Moody's revivalist meetings.

In 1880, Guiteau turned his attention to Republican politics. During this time, the Republican party was undergoing tremendous internal strife and had split into two factions: one was the Stalwarts, led by Roscoe Conkling; the other was the Half-Breeds, led by James G. Blaine. The Half-Breeds candidate, James A. Garfield, had been elected to the presidency in 1880. Initially, Guiteau supported the Stalwarts, but later changed sides. Guiteau moved to Washington, D.C. seeking an appointed office from Secretary of State James G. Blaine. Blaine ignored him, and Guiteau changed sides again; this time backing the Stalwarts. By the middle of May 1881, Guiteau decided to assassinate the President. By mid-June, he produced a rambling before-the-fact explanation for his actions, sending the letter to General William T. Sherman.

The wife and daughter of President Garfield had spent a miserable spring. Ill and exceedingly uncomfortable as the heat of summer arrived in Washington, the family left for the shores of New Jersey, with the President to follow. On July 2, 1881, President James A. Garfield left the White House and proceeded to the Baltimore and Potomac Railroad Station, where he was to board a train to Elberon, New Jersey, and join his vacationing family. As Garfield waited for the train, Guiteau arrived and shot Garfield twice, once in the arm and once in the back. Garfield was to die a slow and lingering death. His doctors probed and probed, often with dirty instruments, in an attempt to locate the bullet which had lodged in the president's back. Even inventor Alexander Graham Bell was called upon to examine the president, using a primitive form of metal detector. Infection caused Garfield's death. Guiteau was arrested and sent to the District of Columbia Jail. His seven-month trial was marked by pleas of insanity from both his lawyers and his family. The pleas were rejected, and Guiteau was convicted and sentenced to be executed. On June 30, 1882, Charles Guiteau was hanged.

Name ____________________

Date ____________________

Guiteau Plans to Kill the President

Read the two excerpts from the correspondence of Charles Guiteau. Be prepared to discuss them.

Letter from Charles Guiteau to General William T. Sherman

To General Sherman: I have just shot the President. I shot him several times as I wished him to go as easily as possible. His death was a political necessity. I am a lawyer, theologian, and politician. I am a stalwart of the Stalwarts. I was with Gen. Grant, and the rest of our men in New York during the canvass. I am going to the Jail. Please order out your troops and take possession of the Jail at once. Very respectfully, Charles Guiteau.[1]

Affidavit/Address by Guiteau: "To the American People . . ."

Washington June 16, 1881. To the American People: I conceived the idea of removing the President four weeks ago. Not a soul knew of my purpose. I conceived the idea myself and kept it to myself. I read the newspapers carefully for and against the Administration, and gradually the conviction settled on me that the President's removal was a political necessity, because he proved a traitor to the men that made him, and thereby imperilled [sic] the life of the Republic. . . . This is not murder. It is a political necessity.[2]

[1]Correspondence: Charles Guiteau to William T. Sherman, July 1881 in the Charles Guiteau Collection, Georgetown University Library.

[2]Affidavit/Address by Guiteau: "To the American People . . ." 16 June 1881 in the Charles Guiteau Collection, Georgetown University Library.

Name ____________________

Date ____________________

"A Bright Image Dimmed with Time"

Read the following information. Then read the newspaper accounts of Garfield's last moments and death and the memorial poem that appeared at the time of Garfield's death. Be prepared for discussion.

The presidential administration of James A. Garfield lasted two hundred days from inauguration to death. Born into rural poverty in a log cabin, Garfield was to hold offices ranging from minister of the Disciples of Christ, president of Hiram College, lawyer, and the youngest major general in the U.S. Army during the Civil War. He resigned his military commission in 1863 to run for a seat in the U.S. House of Representatives. Admired by many, Garfield was supported by such notable figures as Horatio Alger, who wrote a widely distributed biography of Garfield. Garfield was an intellectual who recognized the problems of the newly industrialized nation. He had many friends in the Republican Party and was admired equally by the Democrats. In 1880, he was elected to the U.S. Senate from his home state, Ohio. That same year, a deadlocked Republican presidential convention saw the nomination of Garfield on the thirty-sixth ballot. In November 1880, Garfield was elected President, defeating Winfield Scott Hancock by less than ten thousand popular votes. Garfield immediately entered into a patronage struggle with Roscoe Conklin. When Garfield was assassinated by Charles Guiteau, many believed that this struggle was at the root of Guiteau's behavior. Modern research has shown that while Guiteau did seek appointed office from Garfield, the assassination resulted from Guiteau's obsession with Republican politics and his mental illness. When Garfield died as a result of his wounds in September 1881, the nation was plunged into mourning. Americans had followed closely newspaper accounts of Garfield's struggle to survive.

The End: Death Comes Suddenly—The Last Sad Scenes—
How the Lamp of Light Went Out
By Associated Press to the Plain Dealer

Elberon, [New Jersey,] September 20.—Up to ten o'clock last night there was no apprehension of immediate danger. Everything seemed indicative of a quiet night at 10:30. While Dr. Boynton was conversing at the Elberon, a messenger suddenly appeared and spoke to the doctor in an undertone, and the doctor immediately left the table at which he was sitting and started on a run for the Francklyn cottage [where Garfield was being treated]. This movement was a signal to the representatives of the press congregated at the hotel that something unusual had occurred. But a few moments elapsed when Mr. Warren Young, one of the executive clerks, came to the Elberon Hotel and announced the President was dead.

Previous to his death the only words spoken by the President were that he had a severe pain in his head. It is supposed by the surgeons that death was occasioned by a clot of blood forming in the heart. [An autopsy would show that Garfield suffered from a massive infection.] Dr. Bliss was the first one notified of the President's expression of pain, and upon entering the room he at once saw that the end was near. The members of his family were immediately summoned to the bedside, and all arrived.

Mrs. Garfield bore the trying ordeal with great fortitude, and exhibited unprecedented courage. She gave way to no paroxysms of grief, and after death became evident she quietly withdrew to her own room. There she sat full of grief, but with too much courage to exhibit it to those around her. She was laboring under a terrible strain, and despite her efforts tears flowed from her eyes, and her lips became drawn by her noble attempt to bear the burden with which she had been afflicted. Miss Mollie [Garfield's daughter] was greatly affected and bursts of tears flowed from the child's eyes, notwithstanding her noble effort to follow the example of her mother.

Name ______________________

Date ______________________

The Death Scene was one never to be forgotten. Perfect quiet prevailed and there was not a murmur heard while the President was sinking. After death had been pronounced the body was properly arranged by Dr. S. A. Boynton.[3]

The Official Bulletin

Elberon, Sept. 20, 1:15 A.M.—The following official bulletin has just been issued:
Elberon, N. J. September 19, 1881, 11:36 P.M.

The President died at 10:35 p.m. After the bulletin was issued at 5:30 this evening the President continued in much the same condition as during the afternoon, the pulse varying from 102 to 104, with a rather increased force and volume. After taking nourishment he fell into a quiet sleep. About thirty-five minutes before his death, and while asleep, the pulse rose to 120, and was somewhat more feeble. At ten minutes after ten o'clock he awoke, complaining of a severe pain over the region of the heart, and almost immediately became unconscious, and ceased to breathe at 10:35.

[Signed]

D. W. Briss
F. H. Hamilton
D. Hayes Agnew[4]

A Nation Mourns

Americans were transfixed by grief at the death of President Garfield, even though he was personally unknown to a majority of Americans. There was an outpouring of personal tributes, which appeared in newspapers across the country. During the Victorian era, people often expressed their grief in poetic form. Below is an example.

At Elberon

by Tracy Hempstead

After so long a time! Merciful Father
    Pity the land where the dead ruler lies!
Vainly she utters her sorrow increasing,
    Earthwardly bending her tear-burdened eyes.

Dead in the prime of his manhood and luster;
    Dead at the crest of his worthy-won fame;
Leaving enwreathed in the hearts of his people
    Forever the light of an undying name.

Grandly he wrought in the world's sturdy battle;
    Grandly he scaled honor's dizziest height,
Then, as an eagle would heavenward ascending,
    Passed into clouds and was lost to the sight.

Breathless the nation has watched o'er his pillow,
    Praying—oh never was earnester made!
Hoping—heart weary, yet hoping unshaken
    Still, that the death angel's hand might be stayed.

[3]"The End," *The Plain Dealer*, 20 September 1881.
[4]"The Official Bulletin," *The Plain Dealer*, 24 September 1881.

Name ______________________

Date ______________________

Through the long days of the fierce flaming summer,
Far into autumn time, bravely strove he,
Only to sink in the grasp of the victor,
There by the shores of the low-moaning sea.

Bury him, then, with the whole people weeping!
Toll the slow bell in its mournfullest tone!
Weep with the widowed one; weep for the fatherless!
Our's is a grief like a kinsman were gone.

Muffle the drum, and with low drooping banners
Bear home the soldier chief, gone to his rest.
There let him sleep, the loved of his country,
Close by that land-bounded sea of the west.

Little Rock, Ark., September 20, 1881.[5]

[5]*The Plain Dealer*, 26 September 1881.

Name ____________________

Date ____________________

The Pendleton Act of 1883

The Pendleton Act was passed in 1883 as a direct response to the assassination of President James A. Garfield. Below are excerpts from the law. Read them, and be prepared for class discussion.

First, for open, competitive examinations for testing the fitness of applicants for the public service now classified or to be classified hereunder. Such examinations shall be practical in their character, and . . . shall relate to those matters which will fairly test the relative capacity and the fitness of the persons examined to discharge the duties of the service into which they seek to be appointed.

. . . [A]ll the offices, places, and employments so arranged or to be arranged in classes shall be filled by selections according to grade from among those graded highest as the results of such competitive examinations. . . .

. . . [T]here shall be a period of probation before any absolute appointment or employment. . . .

. . . [N]o person in the public service is . . . under any obligations to contribute to any political fund, or to render any political service . . . he will not be removed or otherwise prejudiced for refusing to do so.

. . . [N]o person in said service has any right to use his official authority or influence to coerce the political action of any person or body. . . .

. . . [W]ithin sixty days after the passage of this act it shall be the duty of the Secretary of the Treasury . . . to arrange in classes the several clerks and persons employed by the collector, naval officer, surveyor, and appraisers, or either of them, . . . at their respective offices in each customs district where the whole number of said clerks and persons shall be all together as many as fifty. . . .

Within said sixty days it shall be the duty of the Postmaster-General . . . to separately arrange in classes the several clerks and persons employed, or in the public service, at each post-office, or under any postmaster of the United States, where the whole number of said clerks and persons shall together amount to as many as fifty. . . .

. . . That after the expiration of six months from the passage of this act no officer or clerk shall be appointed, and no person shall be employed to enter or be promoted in either of the said classes now existing . . . until he has passed an examination, or is shown to be specially exempted from such examination in conformity herewith . . . [N]othing herein contained shall be construed to take from those honorably discharged from the military or naval service any preference conferred . . . nor shall any officer not in the executive branch of the government, or any person merely employed as a laborer or workman, be required to be classified hereunder; nor, unless by direction of the Senate, shall any person who has been nominated for confirmation by the Senate be required to be classified or to pass an examination.

. . . [W]henever there are already two or more members of a family in the public service in the grades covered by this act, no other member of such family shall be eligible to appointment to any of said grades.

. . . [N]o recommendation of any person who shall apply for office or place under the provisions of this Act which may be given by any Senator or member of the House of Representatives, except as to the character or residence of the applicant, shall be received or considered by any person concerned in making any examination or appointment under this act.

Name ______________________

Date ______________________

. . . [N]o Senator, or Representative, or Territorial Delegate of the Congress, or Senator, Representative, or Delegate elect, or any officer or employee of either of said houses, and no executive, judicial, military, or naval officer of the United States, shall, directly or indirectly, solicit or receive or be in any manner concerned in soliciting or receiving, any assessment, subscription, or contribution for any political purpose whatever, from any officer, clerk, or employee of the United States, or any department, branch, or bureau thereof, or from any person receiving any salary or compensation from moneys derived from the Treasury of the United States.

. . . [N]o person shall . . . in the discharge of official duties by any officer or employee of the United States mentioned in this act, on in any navy-yard, fort, or arsenal, solicit in any manner whatever, or receive any contribution of money or any other thing of value for any political purpose whatever.

Marching to Glory: The Founding of the Salvation Army in America

Objectives

- To become familiar with the relationship between the Methodist Episcopal Church and the Salvation Army
- To examine and analyze the relationship between the doctrines of the Methodist Episcopal Church and those of the Salvation Army

Notes to the Teacher

During the eighteenth and nineteenth centuries, religious reform movements flourished in America and Europe. Reformers sought to increase the influence of the laity in church affairs, make religious doctrine more accessible to church members, and reflect new interests in salvation. The Methodist Church was established by John and Charles Wesley as a reform movement in the Anglican Church during the mid-eighteenth century. More than a hundred years later, Charles Booth, a Methodist minister who worked among the poor of London's East End, founded the Salvation Army.

In this lesson, students discuss the formation of the Methodist Episcopal Church and the Salvation Army in America, read selections from the Methodist Discipline of 1808 and the Doctrine of the Salvation Army, 1878, and compare and contrast in an essay the religious doctrines of both, examining the relationship between the two churches.

Reminder to Teachers

- Decide if the appropriate primary sources analysis worksheets from the appendix will be used in this lesson.
- Assign those sections of the basal textbook that are relevant to this lesson.

Procedure

1. Ask students to define *reform* (*to change for the better*). Explain that religious institutions have throughout time been subject to reform movements. Ask students for examples (*Martin Luther, John Calvin, the Great Awakening, George Fox, Mother Ann Lee*). Explain that often new religions are formed as offshoots of other more established religions, usually when members of a church differ with church leadership or raise questions regarding doctrinal beliefs. Use the split between the Catholic Church and the Orthodox Church or the split between the Anglican Church and the Quakers as examples. Distribute **Handout 22**, and have students read it and complete the questions for discussion. Review students' responses.

Suggested Responses:

1. *The church wrote a constitution, created a publishing house, and set up a program of revivalism and camp meetings.*
2. *They were to avoid evil, do good, and use the means of grace supplied by God.*
3. *The split was caused by the antislavery views of the northern members of the conference.*
4. *The two issues were the role of women and the laity in the church.*
5. *The changes were the rise in the social gospel, the holiness movement, liberal theology, and pacifism, and a revival of the temperance movement.*
6. *Booth was a Methodist preacher and his wife, Catherine, was the daughter of a Methodist lay leader.*
7. *It was rooted in the Methodist doctrine of holiness.*
8. *The doctrine asked church members to make an active commitment to God, which led to sanctification, and to help others to be transformed by a spiritual life.*
9. *Women were the equal of men and entitled to preach.*
10. *The Salvation Army helped the unchurched poor by preaching for salvation and against drink, helping the ill and dying, and providing programs for children, youths, and women.*

2. Stress the connection between the Methodist Episcopal Church and the Salvation Army. Distribute **Handout 23**. Have students read the material in part A and complete the matching activity in part B. Review the instructions, and explain that some of the articles may be used more than once. Review students' responses.

   Suggested Responses, Part B.

   Doctrine 1—*Article V*

   Doctrine 2—*Article I*

   Doctrine 3—*Article IV*

   Doctrine 4—*Article II*

   Doctrine 5—*Article VII*

   Doctrine 6—*Article II*

   Doctrine 7—*Article XII*

   Doctrine 8—*Article IX*

   Doctrine 9—*Article XVI*

   Doctrine 10—*Article XII*

3. Have students use the information contained in the handouts to complete the following essay question: The Salvation Army had its roots in the Methodist Church. Discuss the founding of the Methodist Episcopal Church and the Salvation Army and compare and contrast the doctrinal beliefs of the two religious institutions. Have selected students share their essays.

Extension Activities

1. Have students research and prepare reports on other religious revivals in America, such as the Shakers; the Seventh Day Adventists; the Utopian communities of Oneida, New York, and Amana, Iowa; and the revivalists of the early 1920s, such as Billy Sunday and Aimee Semple McPherson.

2. Have students research and report on the Methodist circuit riders, who spread the gospel among America's frontier settlers.

Name ______________________

Date ______________________

The Methodists and Salvation Army

Read this resource sheet, and answer the questions for discussion.

In 1736, John Wesley and his brother Charles came to the English colony of Georgia as Anglican missionaries. In less than a year, they returned to England, disillusioned and discouraged. In May 1738, John Wesley underwent a religious experience, which led him to seek a renewal within the Anglican Church. Out of this renewal grew the Methodist lay movement, and in 1769, Wesley sent two lay preachers, Richard Boardman and Joseph Pilmore, to the colonies. In 1771, Francis Asbury, who was to shape Methodism in America, arrived. By 1773, the first conference of lay preachers was held in America. Attendees emphasized a strong discipline among societies [church congregations] and preachers and set up a schedule of regular conferences for preachers.

John Wesley openly opposed the actions of America's colonists against the British crown, and after America's separation from England, changes had to be made in American Methodism. Thomas Coke was sent to bring the Sunday Service of the Methodists to North America. This brought changes to America in the Thirty-nine Articles of the Anglican Church that had provided the format for worship used by the Weslyans. In 1784, the Methodist leadership in America met at the Lovely Lane Chapel in Baltimore, Maryland, and established the Methodist Episcopal Church in America. In attendance was Richard Allen, an African-American minister from Philadelphia. Because of mistreatment, Allen eventually left the Methodist Episcopal Church and founded the African Episcopal Methodist Church in 1816.

In 1808, the Methodist Episcopal Conference established the church's first constitution, created a publishing house, and set up a program of revivalism and camp meetings. The church's general rules exhorted its members to avoid evil, do good, and use the means of grace supplied by God. Organized around classes led by lay leaders, the Methodist Episcopal Church thrived during the early part of the nineteenth century. Ordained preachers, sent out by church bishops, traveled a circuit among the often far-flung churches of America's spreading frontier. Visiting every month or every other month, these preachers brought the gospel and created the first lay administered Sunday schools, which served as the principal source of prospective church members.

One of the aims of the church was an extension of the antislavery beliefs of its founder, John Wesley. By 1844, the beliefs of the northern and southern sections of the church were so far apart that the church split in two, creating two conferences. The new Methodist Episcopal Church, South, wrote a church discipline for its southern slaveholding members. During the ensuing Civil War, the Southern Conference suffered tremendous losses. Many churches were destroyed or in ruins by the end of the war, a third of its membership lost their lives, clergy were killed or wounded in the war, and educational and publishing programs were damaged.

In 1870, the General Conference of the Methodist Episcopal Church, South, transferred all African-American members to the newly established Colored Methodist Episcopal Church, in effect creating a segregated Methodist Church in the South. The period from 1890 to 1920 saw prosperous times for the church. By 1890, the Methodist Episcopal Church had four million members. Home missions were established in urban as well as rural areas, and theological seminaries were founded to educate the future church leadership. Overseas missions were established in Asia, Europe, Africa, and Latin America.

Two major issues dominated church conference meetings at this time—the role of lay representation in the church and the role of women. The Methodist Church in England had granted lay representatives a voice in conference meetings beginning in 1830. The Methodist Episcopal Church in America and its affiliated churches, the Evangelical Association and Church of the United Brethren in Christ, did not grant this right until 1932. Women were not allowed to serve as delegates until 1892 in the Methodist Episcopal Church and 1922 in the Methodist Episcopal Church, South. Church mission societies were often the only outlet for women within the formal church organization. Interestingly, women were allowed to serve as administrators in both the foreign and U.S. missions, but

Name ____________________

Date ____________________

the ordination of women as ministers was not permitted until 1889, and in the Methodist Episcopal Church, South, not until 1939.

The period between the Civil War and World War I saw changes in the theological structure of the church. The advent of the Social Gospel, the holiness movement and the rise of liberal theology, together with the advocacy of pacifism among the church's leadership led to controversy. A revival in the temperance movement led to the publication of tracts and the support of abstinence pledges among church members.

In 1865, William Booth, a preacher, who had converted to Methodism at the age of fifteen, was administering a "Christian Mission" in the slums of London. Booth struggled in obscurity, doing evangelical and social welfare work among the poor of the East End. His work was often the subject of scorn and ridicule. A revival held in July 1865 saw Booth and his followers stoned by an angry mob in the East End. He and his wife, Catherine Mumford Booth, the daughter of a lay Methodist leader, eventually became involved in a Methodist reform movement. Booth became a follower of the Chartists' social and political reform. Both William and Catherine Booth had alcoholic parents, which led to a strong temperance component in their religious work. In 1878, Booth reorganized his mission along quasi-military lines and renamed it the "Volunteer Army in the War against Sin." When Catherine Booth and their son Bramwell objected to being considered "a volunteer" in a fight they believed was a calling in life, Booth changed the name of the organization to the Salvation Army.

The theological beliefs of the new army had its roots in Methodism's Doctrine of Holiness[1] and were shaped by Catherine Booth. Based on the preaching of Phoebe Palmer, a New York lay evangelist who preached in England, the doctrine was based on John Wesley's doctrine of "holiness." These beliefs called for a second baptism, which would represent an active commitment to the Lord, leading to sanctification. God would replace man's inner sin with spiritual love and members of "God's Army" were to help others experience this transformation. Encouraged to testify publicly about their conversion, members were instructed to embrace the selfless tasks, which were needed to care for the poor. Women were active participants in Booth's new army. Catherine believed that women who received an education equal to that of men were the intellectual equals of those men. She believed that women had spiritual authority from God and were as entitled to preach as men.

Booth became the "general," and his followers were given military ranks and titles. A "War Congress" produced a standardized uniform of dark blue with red trim, which members wore in their fight against sin and the devil.

By 1880, a branch was established in the slums of New York City's Hell's Kitchen. Army members sought out the unchurched. Using popular music, lively pageantry, and dramatic testimony from new members, the Army preached a gospel structured around the themes of love of God, service to others, and salvation. The "Lads and Lassies" of the Army quickly became a common sight on the streets of New York preaching for salvation and against drink, ministering to the ill and dying, providing programs for children, youth, and women, and encouraging members to seek perfection with God's help.[2]

[1]*Official Website of The United Methodist Church*, <http://www.umc.org> (2 October 2000).
[2]Information for this handout is from the *Official Website of The United Methodist Church* <http://www.umc.org> and *Marching to Glory: The History of the Salvation Army in the United States, 1880–1992*, E. H. McKinley, (Grand Rapids, Mich.: William B. Eerdmans Publishing Co., 1995).

Name ______________________

Date ______________________

1. What actions taken by the Methodist Episcopal Church in 1808 established the church as a viable entity in America?

2. What were the basic beliefs of Methodism?

3. What caused the split in the Methodist Episcopal Church during the mid-nineteenth century?

4. What two issues dominated the Methodist Episcopal Church after 1900?

5. What changes took place in the theological structure of the church between the Civil War and World War I?

6. What was William Booth's connection to Methodism?

7. In what was the Salvation Army rooted?

8. What was the doctrine of holiness?

9. What was the Salvation Army's position towards women?

10. What group was targeted by the Salvation Army for help? What type of help was provided?

Name ______________________

Date ______________________

Doctrinal Standards and General Rules of the Methodist Church

Part A.

Below are excerpts from the *Doctrinal Standards and General Rules of the Methodist Church* as they appeared in the text of the 1808 constitution of the Methodist Church. These standards were amended in 1848 and again in 1868. Read the selection.

Article I—Of Faith in the Holy Trinity

There is but one living and true God, everlasting, without body or parts, of infinite power, wisdom, and goodness; the maker and preserver of all things, both visible and invisible. And in unity of this Godhead there are three persons, of one substance, power, and eternity—the Father, the Son, and the Holy Ghost.

Article II—Of the Word, or Son of God, Who Was Made Very Man

The Son, who is the Word of the Father, the very and eternal God, of one substance with the Father, took man's nature in the womb of the blessed Virgin; so that two whole and perfect natures, that is to say, the Godhead and Manhood, were joined together in one person, never to be divided, whereof is one Christ, very God and very Man, who truly suffered, was crucified, dead, and buried, to reconcile his Father to us, and to be a sacrifice, not only for original guilt, but also for actual sins of men. . . .

Article IV—Of the Holy Ghost

The Holy Ghost, proceeding from the Father and the Son, is of one substance, majesty, and glory with the Father and the Son, very and eternal God.

Article V—Of the Sufficiency of the Holy Scriptures for Salvation

The Holy Scripture containeth all things necessary to salvation; so that whatsoever is not read therein, nor may be proved thereby, is not to be required of any man that it should be believed as an article of faith, or be thought requisite or necessary to salvation. . . .

Article VII—Of Original or Birth Sin

Original sin standeth not in the following of Adam . . . , but it is the corruption of the nature of every man, that naturally is engendered of the offspring of Adam, whereby man is very far gone from original righteousness, and of his own nature inclined to evil, and that continually. . . .

Article IX—Of the Justification of Man

We are accounted righteous before God only for the merit of our Lord and Saviour Jesus Christ, by faith, and not for our own works or deservings. Wherefore, that we are justified by faith, only, is a most wholesome doctrine, and very full of comfort. . . .

Name ___________________________

Date ___________________________

Article XII—Of Sin after Justification

Not every sin willingly committed after justification is the sin against the Holy Ghost, and unpardonable. Wherefore, the grant of repentance is not to be denied to such as fall into sin after justification. After we have received the Holy Ghost, we may depart from grace given, and fall into sin, and, by the grace of God, rise again and amend our lives. And therefore they are to be condemned who say they can no more sin as long as they live here; or deny the place of forgiveness to such as truly repent. . . .

Article XVI—Of the Sacraments

Sacraments ordained of Christ are not only badges or tokens of Christian men's profession, but rather they are certain signs of grace, and God's good will toward us. . . . There are two Sacraments ordained of Christ our Lord in the Gospel; that is to say Baptism and the Supper of the Lord. . . .[3]

[3]"The Articles of Religion of the Methodist Church," *Official Website of The United Methodist Church*, <http://www.umc.org/churchlibrary/discipline/doctrinalstandards/doctrinal_standards.htm> (2 October 2000).

Name ______________________

Date ______________________

Part B.

The document below was set forth in the Deed Poll of 1878. Using the information in part A, match the Articles of Faith of the Methodist Episcopal Church with the Doctrines of the Salvation Army. Write the article number in the space provided. Some articles may be used more than once.

The Doctrines of the Salvation Army

__________ 1. We believe that the Scriptures of the Old and New Testaments were given by inspiration of God; and that they only constitute the divine rule of Christian faith and practice.

__________ 2. We believe there is only one God, who is infinitely perfect—the Creator, Preserver, and Governor of all things—and who is the only proper object of religious worship.

__________ 3. We believe that there are three persons in the Godhead—the Father, the Son, and the Holy Ghost—undivided in essence and co-equal in power and glory.

__________ 4. We believe that in the person of Jesus Christ the divine and human natures are united; so that He is truly and properly God, and truly and properly man.

__________ 5. We believe that our first parents were created in a state of innocence but, by their disobedience, they lost their purity and happiness; and that in consequence of their fall all men have become sinners, totally depraved, and as such are justly exposed to the wrath of God.

__________ 6. We believe that the Lord Jesus Christ has, by his suffering and death, made an atonement for the whole world, so that whosoever will may be saved.

__________ 7. We believe that repentance toward God, faith in our Lord Jesus Christ, and regeneration by the Holy Spirit are necessary to salvation.

__________ 8. We believe that we are justified by grace, through faith in our Lord Jesus Christ; and that he that believeth hath the witness in himself.

__________ 9. We believe that continuance in a state of salvation depends upon continued obedient faith in Christ.

__________ 10. We believe that it is the privilege of all believers to be "wholly sanctified," and that their "whole spirit and soul and body" may "be preserved blameless unto the coming of our Lord Jesus Christ" (I Thessalonians 5:23).[4]

[4]"The Doctrines of The Salvation Army," 1878 in *Marching to Glory: The History of the Salvation Army in the United States, 1880–1992*, E. H. McKinley (Grand Rapids, Mich.: William B. Eerdmans Publishing Co., 1995), 351–52.

Women in the Workforce of the West

Objectives

- To examine the role of women in the workforce during the settlement of the American West
- To assess the variety of occupations performed by women during the nineteenth century in the American West

Notes to the Teacher

Women were the glue that held the settlements of the West together. Frequently, they were the only connection with the more civilized East. Women promoted the establishment of schools and churches, supported the temperance movement, and worked alongside their husbands in the fields as they attempted to scratch a living out of an often relentlessly savage frontier. They buried their children—often in unbelievable numbers—made quilts, canned food, and often served as dentist and doctor as they raised their families and carved out a home in the wilderness. Some women, like Marthy Jane Cannary, assumed the guise of a man, and performed jobs that were usually reserved for men. Others followed a more traditional path, such as operating a restaurant. Professional women, doctors, lawyers, teachers, and dentists also settled on the western frontier. Women performed on the fringes of proper society when they performed in theaters. Women occupied a substantial place in the frontier workforce. Without them, the American frontier would have developed very differently.

In this lesson, students read and analyze an excerpt from the autobiography of Marthy Jane Cannary, better known as Calamity Jane, and examine and analyze a selection of documents that illustrate the variety of occupations performed by women in the American West.

Reminder to Teachers

- Decide if the appropriate primary sources analysis worksheets from the appendix will be used in this lesson.
- Assign those sections of the basal textbook that are relevant to this lesson.

Procedure

1. Discuss the role of women in nineteenth-century society; use the Notes to the Teacher as a guide. Explain to students that life on the frontier of the West often saw women in roles which were traditionally male in the East. Ask students for examples of similar roles in today's society. (*Some religions, such as Catholicism or the Mormons, do not permit women to act as priests or ministers; women do not compete against men in certain professional sports, such as baseball, football, or hockey.*)

2. Distribute **Handout 24.** Have students read the excerpt and complete the questions for discussion. Review students' responses.

   Suggested Responses:

   1. *She grew up outdoors and had a fondness for horses and adventure.*
   2. *She wore men's clothing and adopted the disguise of a man.*
   3. *She rescued Captain Egan, who had been wounded during an Indian attack.*
   4. *She acted as a pony express rider between Deadwood and Custer, South Dakota.*
   5. *She was a quick shot and an excellent rider.*
   6. *She went after his killer with a meat cleaver and saw that he was imprisoned and later hanged.*
   7. *She traveled all across the West and held a variety of jobs, including rancher and hotel operator.*
   8. *When she returned to Deadwood, all the citizens of the town wanted to hear about her adventures; Eastern gentlemen convinced her that there was a market for her autobiography.*

3. Ask students for examples of nontraditional jobs women might have held in the nineteenth century West (*doctor, dentist, barber, restaurant owner, banker*). Distribute **Handout 25.** Divide the class into six groups, and assign each group one illustration to examine. Have students complete the questions for the group's illustration. Allow about

fifteen minutes for students to complete this task. Rearrange students into six new groups, making sure that each group has one member from each of the previous six groups. Have students share the answers from each of the original groups.

Suggested Responses:

Fig. 10.1.

1. *restaurant advertisement*
2. *Nellie Cashman/newspaper advertisement*
3. *restaurant owner*
4. *Women owned businesses.*

Fig. 10.2.

1. *theater handbill*
2. *advertisement for appearance by local actress*
3. *actress*
4. *Theater was an acceptable profession.*

Fig. 10.3.

1. *dentist's advertisement*
2. *Dr. Frances Treadwell*
3. *dentist*
4. *Women practiced professions usually reserved for men.*

Fig. 10.4.

1. *Wells Fargo Co. agent's certificate*
2. *certificate issued to Carrie Hill*
3. *Wells Fargo express agent*
4. *Women held positions of trust.*

Fig. 10.5.

1. *homestead deed*
2. *issued by federal land office*
3. *farmer*
4. *Women could own property.*

Fig. 10.6.

1. *Teacher's certificate*
2. *issued by county school superintendent*
3. *teacher*
4. *Women worked as teachers and were as well educated as men.*

4. To conclude, have each group reach consensus on why it was important for women in the West to assume roles usually assigned to men. Have each group share its conclusion.

Extension Activities

1. Have selected students research and report on other women who assumed men's roles in the settlement of the American West.
2. Have students research and prepare a presentation on a famous woman in the American West.

Name ______________________

Date ______________________

The Life and Adventures of Calamity Jane

Marthy Jane Cannary was probably the most colorful woman to occupy a space in the history of Western America. She was, at various times, a stagecoach driver, muleskinner, army scout, innkeeper, rancher, and pony express rider. She wrote an autobiographical "dime novel," the equivalent to our modern-day tabloids, in which she recounted her adventures. Read the following excerpts, and answer the questions for discussion.

My maiden name was Marthy Cannary. I was born in Princeton, Missouri, May 1st, 1852. Father and mother were natives of Ohio. I had two brothers and three sisters, I being the oldest of the children. As a child I always had a fondness for adventure and out-door exercise and especial fondness for horses which I began to ride at an early age and continued to do so until I became an expert rider being able to ride the most vicious and stubborn of horses, in fact the greater portion of my life in early times was spent in this manner. . . .

. . . Joined General Custer as a scout at Fort Russell, Wyoming, in 1870, and started for Arizona for the Indian Campaign. Up to this time I had always worn the costume of my sex. When I joined Custer I donned the uniform of a soldier. It was a bit awkward at first but I soon got to be perfectly at home in men's clothes. . . .

After that campaign I returned to Fort Sanders, Wyoming, remained there until spring of 1872, when we were ordered out to the Muscle Shell or Nursey Pursey [Nez Perce] Indian outbreak. In that war Generals Custer, Miles, Terry and Crook were all engaged. This campaign lasted until fall of 1873.

It was during this campaign that I was christened Calamity Jane. It was on Goose Creek, Wyoming, where the town of Sheridan is now located. Capt. Egan was in command of the Post. We were ordered out to quell an uprising of the Indians, and were out for several days, had numerous skirmishes during which six of the soldiers were killed and several severely wounded. When on returning to the Post we were ambushed about a mile and a half from our destination. When fired upon Capt. Egan was shot. I was riding in advance and on hearing the firing turned in my saddle and saw the Captain reeling in his saddle as though about to fall. I turned my horse and galloped back with all haste to his side and got there in time to catch him as he was falling. I lifted him unto my horse in front of me and succeeded in getting him safely to the Fort. Capt. Egan on recovering, laughingly said: "I name you Calamity Jane, the heroine of the plains." I have borne that name up to the present time. . . .

During the month of June I acted as a pony express rider carrying the U.S. mail between Deadwood [South Dakota] and Custer, a distance of fifty miles, over one of the roughest trails in the Black Hills country. As many of the riders before me had been held up and robbed of their packages, mail and money that they carried, for that was the only means of getting mail and money between these points. It was considered the most dangerous route in the Hills, but as my reputation as a rider and quick shot was well known, I was molested very little, for the toll gatherers looked on me as being a good fellow, and they knew that I never missed my mark. I made the round trip every two days which was considered pretty good riding in that country. Remained around Deadwood all that summer visiting all the camps within an area of one hundred miles. My friend, Wild Bill [Hickok], remained in Deadwood during the summer with the exception of occasional visits to the camps. On the 2nd of August [1876], while setting at a gambling table in the Bell Union saloon, in Deadwood, he was shot in the back of the head by the notorious Jack McCall, a desperado. I was in Deadwood at the time and on hearing of the killing

Name ____________________

Date ____________________

made my way at once to the scene of the shooting and found that my friend had been killed by McCall. I at once started to look for the assassin and found him at Shurdy's butcher shop and grabbed a meat cleaver and made him throw up his hands; through the excitement on hearing of Bill's death, having left my weapons on the post of my bed. He was then taken to a log cabin and locked up, well secured as every one thought, but he got away and was afterwards caught at Fagan's ranch on Horse Creek, on the old Cheyenne road and was then taken to Yankton, Dak., where he was tried, sentenced and hung. . . .

In 1881 I went to Wyoming and returned in 1882 to Miles city and took up a ranch on the Yellow Stone, raising stock and cattle, also kept a way side inn, where the weary traveler could be accommodated with food, drink, or trouble if he looked for it. Left the ranch in 1883, went to California, going though the States and territories, reached Ogden the latter part of 1883, and San Francisco in 1884. Left San Francisco in the summer of 1884 for Texas, stopping at Fort Yuma, Arizona, the hottest spot in the United States. Stopping at all the points of interest until I reached El Paso in the fall. While in El Paso, I met Mr. Clinton Burk, a native of Texas, who I married in August 1885. As I thought I had traveled through life long enough alone and thought it was about time to take a partner for the rest of my days. We remained in Texas leading a quiet home life until 1889. On October 18th, 1887, I became the mother of a girl baby, the very image of its father, at least that is what he said, but who has the temper of its mother.

When we left Texas we went to Boulder, Colo., where we kept a hotel until 1893, after which we travelled through Wyoming, Montana, Idaho, Washington, Oregon, and then back to Montana, then to Dakota, arriving in Deadwood October 9th, 1895, after an absence of seventeen years.

My arrival in Deadwood after an absence of so many years created quite an excitement among my many friends of the past, to such an extent that a vast number of the citizens who had come to Deadwood during my absence who had heard so much of Calamity Jane and her many adventures in former years were anxious to see me. Among the many whom I met were several gentlemen from eastern cities who advised me to allow myself to be placed before the public in such a manner as to give the people of the eastern cities an opportunity of seeing the Woman Scout who was made so famous through her daring career in the West and Black Hill countries.[1]

1. What was Marthy Jane Cannary's early life like?

2. How did her life change when she worked as a scout for General Custer?

[1] *The Life and Adventures of Calamity Jane,* Calamity Jane (pseud. Marthy Cannary Burk), original pamphlet edition, 1896, in the collection of the University of Virginia.

Name ______________________

Date ______________________

3. How did she acquire the nickname Calamity Jane?

4. What job did Calamity Jane perform during the month of June?

5. Why was she unmolested?

6. What did Calamity Jane do when Wild Bill Hickok was killed?

7. How did Calamity Jane spend most of her married life?

8. What convinced her to write her autobiography?

Name ____________________

Date ____________________

Women in the West

Women were the glue that held the frontier settlements of the West together. Examine the following visuals, which illustrate the many jobs held by women in the West. Analyze the document assigned to your group by answering these questions:

1. What is the document?
2. Who wrote or issued the document?
3. What profession is illustrated by the document?
4. What does the document tell you about the role of women in the West?

Arcade Restaurant & Chop House

Allen Street, Vizina Block, Tombstone, A. T.

Miss Nellie Cashman, Proprietress.

LATE OF THE DELMONICO, TUCSON.

Meals at All Hours.

Regular Dinner from 4 to 7 p. m. Open Until 8 p. m.

Fig. 10.1.

Fig. 10.1. Arcade restaurant advertisement. Courtesy of the Arizona Historical Society/Tucson. AHS #79325.

Name ______________________

Date ______________________

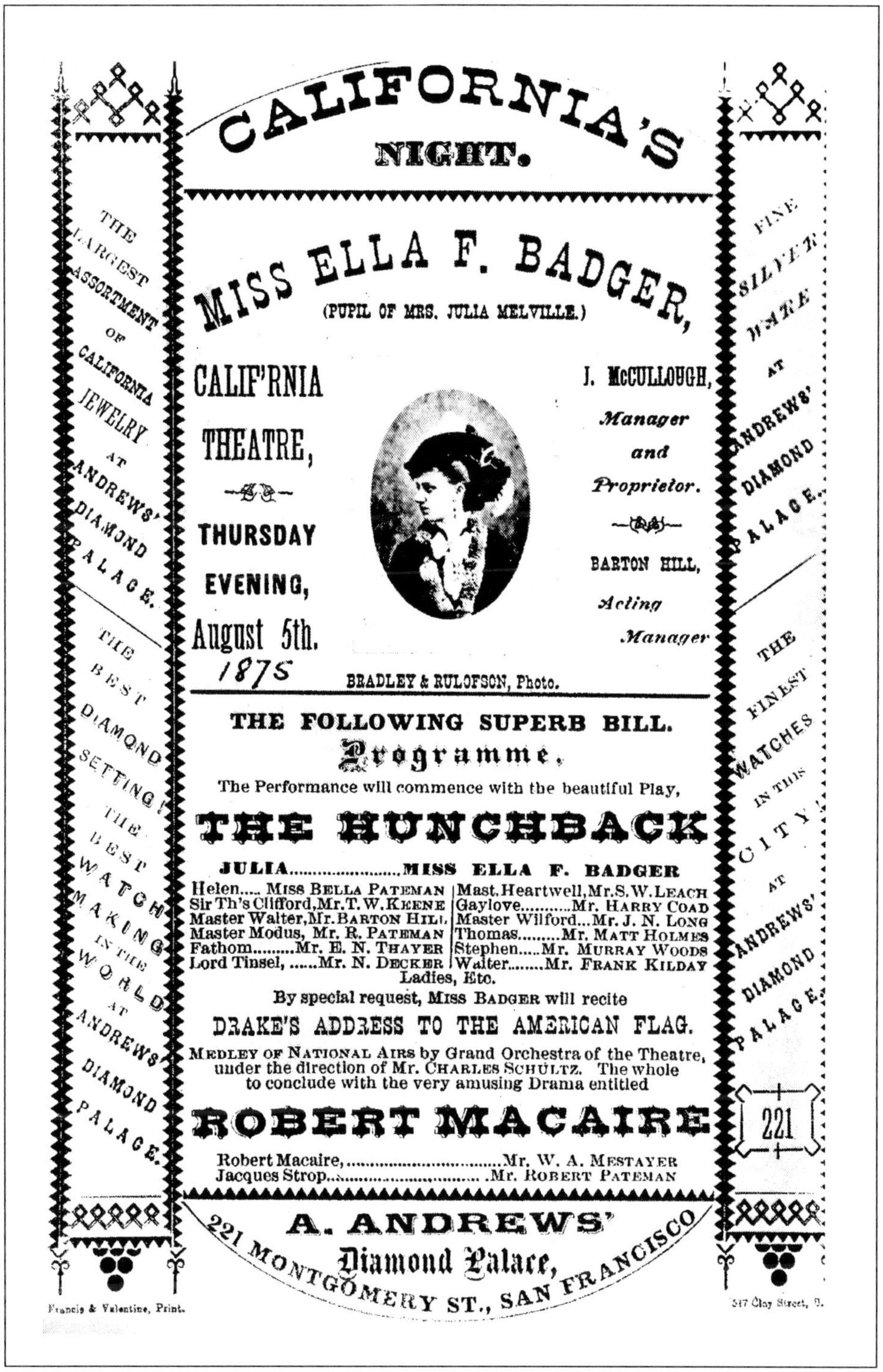

CALIFORNIA'S NIGHT.

MISS ELLA F. BADGER,
(PUPIL OF MRS. JULIA MELVILLE.)

CALIF'RNIA THEATRE,
THURSDAY EVENING,
August 5th.
1875

J. McCULLOUGH,
Manager and Proprietor.

BARTON HILL,
Acting Manager

BRADLEY & RULOFSON, Photo.

THE FOLLOWING SUPERB BILL.
Programme.
The Performance will commence with the beautiful Play,

THE HUNCHBACK

JULIA......................MISS ELLA F. BADGER

Helen..... Miss Bella Pateman	Mast. Heartwell, Mr. S. W. Leach
Sir Th's Clifford, Mr. T. W. Keene	Gaylove..........Mr. Harry Coad
Master Walter, Mr. Barton Hill	Master Wilford...Mr. J. N. Long
Master Modus, Mr. R. Pateman	Thomas.........Mr. Matt Holmes
Fathom.........Mr. E. N. Thayer	Stephen.....Mr. Murray Woods
Lord Tinsel, ...Mr. N. Decker	Walter.......Mr. Frank Kilday

Ladies, Etc.

By special request, Miss Badger will recite
DRAKE'S ADDRESS TO THE AMERICAN FLAG.
Medley of National Airs by Grand Orchestra of the Theatre, under the direction of Mr. Charles Schultz. The whole to conclude with the very amusing Drama entitled

ROBERT MACAIRE

Robert Macaire,...............................Mr. W. A. Mestayer
Jacques Strop...............................Mr. Robert Pateman

A. ANDREWS'
Diamond Palace,
221 MONTGOMERY ST., SAN FRANCISCO

THE LARGEST ASSORTMENT OF CALIFORNIA JEWELRY AT ANDREWS' DIAMOND PALACE.

THE BEST DIAMOND SETTING! THE BEST WATCH MAKING IN THE WORLD AT ANDREWS' DIAMOND PALACE.

FINE SILVER WARE AT ANDREWS' DIAMOND PALACE.

THE FINEST WATCHES IN THIS CITY! AT ANDREWS' DIAMOND PALACE.

221

Francis & Valentine, Print.

517 Clay Street, S.

Fig. 10.2.

Fig. 10.2. Program for "The Hunchback," August 1875. California Historical Society, Theatre Ephemera Collection, North Baker Research Library.

Name ______________________

Date ______________________

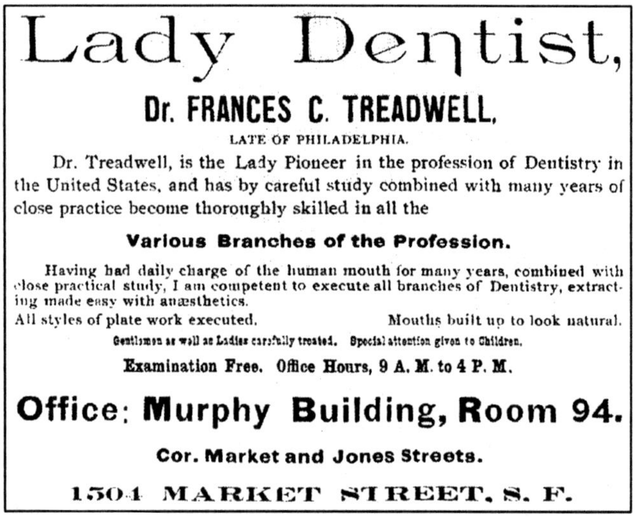

Fig. 10.3.

Fig. 10.4.

Fig. 10.3. Advertisement for Frances C. Treadwell, Lady Dentist from "San Francisco Business Directory," S.F.: San Francisco Directory Company, 1892–94. California Historical Society, North Baker Research Library; FN-23068.

Fig. 10.4. Wells Fargo Agent's Certificate, Cassie Hill, 1884. In the collection of Wells Fargo Bank.

Name ____________________

Date ____________________

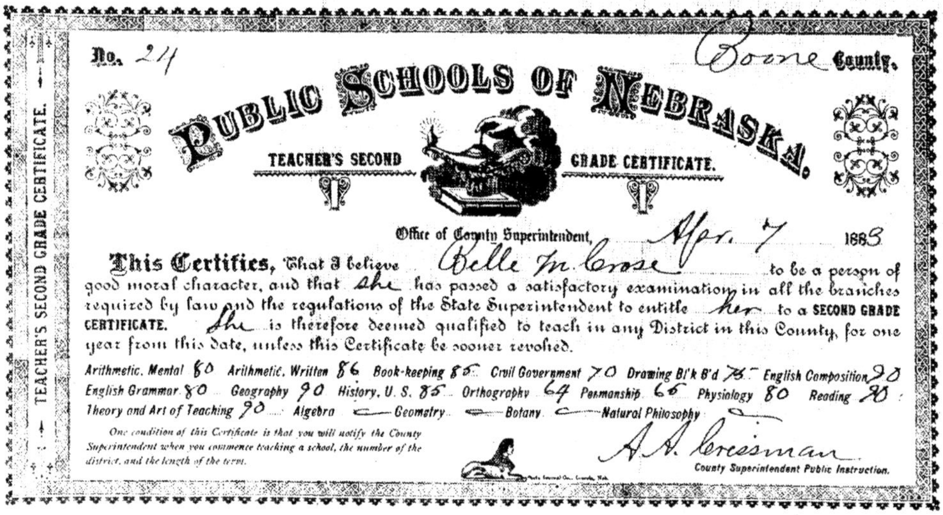

TEACHER'S SECOND GRADE CERTIFICATE.

No. 24 Boone County.

PUBLIC SCHOOLS OF NEBRASKA.

TEACHER'S SECOND GRADE CERTIFICATE.

Office of County Superintendent, Apr. 7 1883

This Certifies, That I believe Belle M. Crose to be a person of good moral character, and that she has passed a satisfactory examination in all the branches required by law and the regulations of the State Superintendent to entitle her to a SECOND GRADE CERTIFICATE. She is therefore deemed qualified to teach in any District in this County, for one year from this date, unless this Certificate be sooner revoked.

Arithmetic, Mental 80 Arithmetic, Written 86 Book-keeping 85 Civil Government 70 Drawing Bl'k B'd 75 English Composition 90 English Grammar 80 Geography 90 History, U. S. 85 Orthography 64 Penmanship 66 Physiology 80 Reading 90 Theory and Art of Teaching 90 Algebra — Geometry — Botany — Natural Philosophy —

One condition of this Certificate is that you will notify the County Superintendent when you commence teaching a school, the number of the district, and the length of the term.

A. A. Cressman
County Superintendent Public Instruction.

Fig. 10.5.

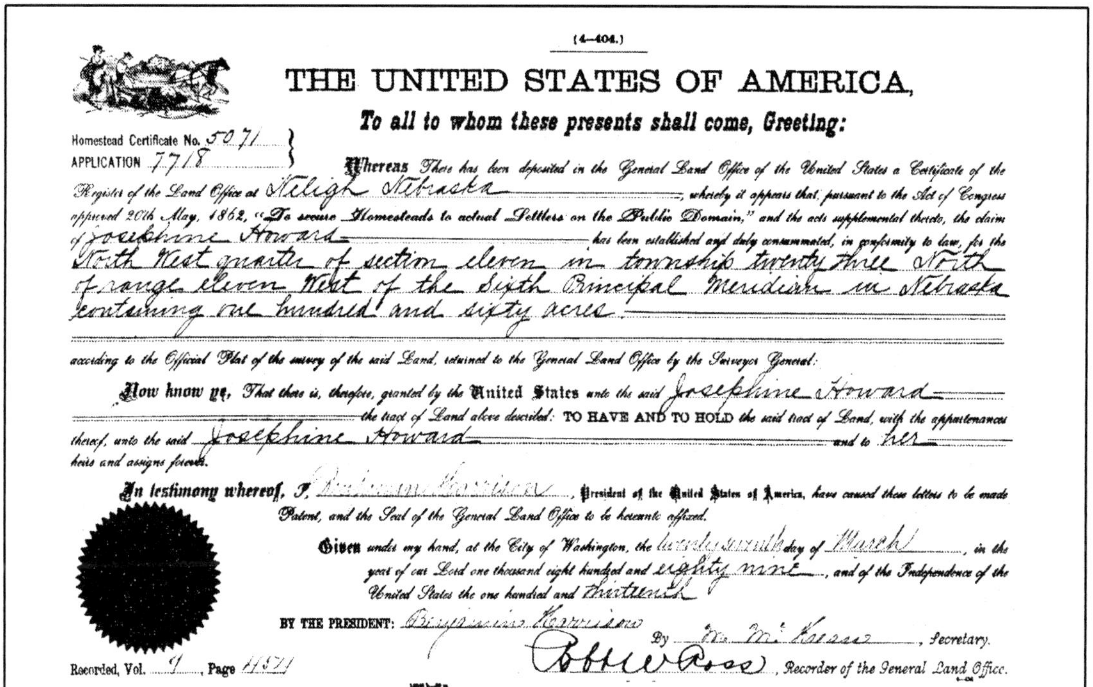

(4—404.)

THE UNITED STATES OF AMERICA,

To all to whom these presents shall come, Greeting:

Homestead Certificate No. 5071
APPLICATION 7718

Whereas There has been deposited in the General Land Office of the United States a Certificate of the Register of the Land Office at Neligh Nebraska, whereby it appears that, pursuant to the Act of Congress approved 20th May, 1862, "To secure Homesteads to actual Settlers on the Public Domain," and the acts supplemental thereto, the claim of Josephine Howard has been established and duly consummated, in conformity to law, for the North West quarter of section eleven in township twenty three North of range eleven West of the Sixth Principal Meridian in Nebraska containing one hundred and sixty acres

according to the Official Plat of the survey of the said Land, returned to the General Land Office by the Surveyor General:

Now know ye, That there is, therefore, granted by the United States unto the said Josephine Howard the tract of Land above described: TO HAVE AND TO HOLD the said tract of Land, with the appurtenances thereof, unto the said Josephine Howard and to her heirs and assigns forever.

In testimony whereof, I, Benjamin Harrison, President of the United States of America, have caused these letters to be made Patent, and the Seal of the General Land Office to be hereunto affixed.

Given under my hand, at the City of Washington, the twenty seventh day of March, in the year of our Lord one thousand eight hundred and eighty nine, and of the Independence of the United States the one hundred and thirteenth

BY THE PRESIDENT: Benjamin Harrison
By M. McKean, Secretary.
Robt W Ross, Recorder of the General Land Office.

Recorded, Vol. 9, Page 4571

Fig. 10.6.

Fig. 10.5. Teaching certificate, Belle M. Crose, 1883. In the collection of the Nebraska State Historical Society.
Fig. 10.6. Homestead deed, Josephine Howard, 1889. In the collection of the Nebraska State Historical Society.

Appendix

Name ____________________

Date ____________________

Written Document Analysis Worksheet*

1. Type of document (check one):

____ Newspaper	____ Map	____ Advertisement
____ Letter	____ Telegram	____ Congressional record
____ Patent	____ Press release	____ Census report
____ Memorandum	____ Report	____ Other ____________

2. Unique physical qualities of the document (check one or more):

____ Interesting letterhead	____ Seals	____ Other ____________
____ Handwritten	____ Notations	
____ Typed	____ "Received" stamp	

3. Date(s) of document: ____________________

4. Author (or creator) of the document: ____________________

   Position (title): ____________________

5. For what audience was the document written? ____________________

6. Document information (There are many possible ways to answer a–e.)

   a. List three things the author said that you think are important.

      1.

      2.

      3.

   b. Why do you think this document was written?

   c. What evidence in the document helps you to know why it was written? Quote from the document.

   d. List two things the document tells you about life in the United States at the time it was written:

      1.

      2.

   e. Write the author a question that is left unanswered by the document.

*Adapted from worksheets developed by the staff of the Education Branch, National Archives, Washington, DC 20408.

Name ________________________

Date ________________________

Map Analysis Worksheet*

1. Type of map (check one):

____ Raised relief map
____ Political map
____ Natural resource map
____ Bird's-eye view
____ Satellite photograph/mosaic
____ Weather map
____ Topographic contour-line map
____ Military map
____ Artifact map
____ Pictograph
____ Other ____________

2. Physical qualities of the map (check one or more):

____ Compass
____ Date
____ Scale
____ Title
____ Legend (key)
____ Handwritten
____ Notations
____ Name of mapmaker
____ Other ____________

3. Date of map: ________________________

4. Creator of map: ________________________

5. Where was the map produced? ________________________

6. Map information

a. List three things in this map that you think are important:

1.

2.

3.

b. Why do you think this map was drawn?

c. What evidence in the map suggests why it was drawn?

d. What information does the map add to the textbook's account of this event?

e. Does the information in this map support or contradict information that you have read about this event? Explain.

f. Write the mapmaker a question that is left unanswered by this map.

*Adapted from worksheets developed by the staff of the Education Branch, National Archives, Washington, DC 20408.

Name ______________________

Date ______________________

Cartoon Analysis Worksheet*

	Visuals	Words (not all cartoons include words)
Step one	1. List the objects or people you see in the cartoon.	1. Identify the cartoon caption and/or title. 2. Locate three words or phrases used by the cartoonist to identify objects or people within the cartoon. 3. Record any important dates or numbers that appear in the cartoon.
Step two	2. Which of the objects on your list are symbols? 3. What do you think each symbol means?	4. Which words or phrases in the cartoon appear to be the most significant? Why do you think so? 5. List adjectives that describe the emotions portrayed in the cartoon.
Step three	a. Describe the action taking place in the cartoon. b. Explain how the words in the cartoon clarify the symbols. c. Explain the message of the cartoon. d. What special interest groups would agree/disagree with the cartoon's message? Why?	

*Adapted from worksheets developed by the staff of the Education Branch, National Archives, Washington, DC 20408.

Name ______________________

Date ______________________

Photograph Analysis Worksheet*

Step 1. Observation

a. Study the photograph for 2 minutes. Form an overall impression of the photograph and then examine individual items. Next, divide the photo into quadrants and study each section to see what new details become visible.

b. Use the chart below to list people, objects, and activities in the photograph.

People	Objects	Activities

Step 2. Inference

Based on what you have observed above, list three things you might infer from this photograph.

Step 3. Questions

a. What questions does this photograph raise in your mind?

b. Where could you find answers to them?

*Adapted from worksheets developed by the staff of the Education Branch, National Archives, Washington, DC 20408.

Name ______________________

Date ______________________

Poster Analysis Worksheet*

1. What is the message of the poster?

2. What is the purpose(s) of the poster?

3. What symbols (if any) are used in the poster?

4. If a symbol is used, is it
   a. clear (easy to interpret)?

   b. memorable?

   c. dramatic?

5. Are the messages in the poster more visual or verbal?

6. Who do you think is the intended audience for the poster?

7. What does the poster hope that the audience will do?

8. The most effective posters use symbols that are unusual, simple, and direct. Is this an effective poster?

*Adapted from worksheets developed by the staff of the Education Branch, National Archives, Washington, DC 20408.

Name ______________________

Date ______________________

Motion Picture Analysis Worksheet*

Step 1. Pre-viewing

a. Title of film: ______________________

Record Group source: ______________________

b. What do you think you will see in this motion picture? List three concepts or ideas that you might expect to see based on the title of the film. List some people you might expect to see based on the title of the film.

Concepts/Ideas	People
1.	1.
2.	2.
3.	3.

Step 2. Viewing

a. Type of motion picture (check where applicable):

_____ Animated cartoon
_____ Newsreel
_____ Theatrical short subject
_____ Combat film
_____ Documentary film
_____ Propaganda film
_____ Training film
_____ Other ______________________

b. Physical qualities of the motion picture (check where applicable):

_____ Music
_____ Special effects
_____ Live action
_____ Animation
_____ Narration
_____ Color
_____ Background noise
_____ Dramatizations

c. Note how camera angles, lighting, music, narration, and/or editing contribute to creating an atmosphere in this film. What is the mood or tone of the film?

*Adapted from worksheets developed by the staff of the Education Branch, National Archives, Washington, DC 20408.

Name ____________________

Date ____________________

Sound Recording Analysis Worksheet*

Step 1. Pre-listening

a. Whose voices will you hear on this recording?

b. What is the date of this recording?

c. Where was this recording made?

Step 2. Listening

a. Type of sound recording (check one):

_____ Policy speech	_____ Arguments before a court	_____ Press conference
_____ News report	_____ Panel discussion	_____ Campaign speech
_____ Entertainment broadcast	_____ Congressional testimony	_____ Other ______________
_____ Convention proceedings	_____ Interview	

b. Unique physical qualities of the recording

_____ Music	_____ Live broadcast	_____ Narrated
_____ Special sound effects	_____ Background sound	

c. What is the tone or mood of this sound recording?

Step 3. Post-listening (or repeated listening)

a. List three things in this sound recording that you think are important:

1.

2.

3.

b. Why do you think the original broadcast was made and for what audience?

c. What evidence in the recording helps you to know why it was made?

*Adapted from worksheets developed by the staff of the Education Branch, National Archives, Washington, DC 20408.

Name ____________________

Date ____________________

Artifact Analysis Worksheet*

1. Physical qualities of the artifact

   Describe the materials from which it was made: bone, pottery, metal, wood, stone, leather, glass, paper, cardboard, cotton, wool, plastic, other material.

2. Special qualities of the artifact

   Describe how it looks and feels: shape, color, texture, size, weight, movable parts, anything printed, stamped, or written on it.

3. Uses of the artifact

   a. What might it have been used for?

   b. Who might have used it?

   c. Where might it have been used?

   d. When might it have been used?

4. What the artifact tells us

   a. What does it tell us about technology of the time in which it was made and used?

   b. What does it tell us about the life and times of the people who made it and used it?

   c. Can you name a similar item used today?

5. Bring the artifact (or a sketch or photograph of the artifact) to class.

*Adapted from worksheets developed by the staff of the Education Branch, National Archives, Washington, DC 20408.

Bibliography

Printed Material

Andronik, Catherine. *Prince of Humbugs: The Life of P. T. Barnum.* New York: Atheneum, 1994.

Cashin, Herchel V., et al. *Under Fire with the Tenth Cavalry.* 1899. Reprint, New York: Arno Press, 1969.

Demarest, David P., Jr. *The River Ran Red: Homestead 1892.* Pittsburgh: University of Pittsburgh Press, 1992.

Galloway, Calvin G. *Our Hearts Fell to the Ground.* Boston: St. Martin's Press, 1995.

Gillett, James B. *Six Years with the Texas Rangers, 1875–1881.* Ed. M. M. Quaife. Lincoln, Nebr.: The University of Nebraska Press, 1925.

Krause, Paul. *The Battle for Homestead, 1880–1892: Politics, Culture, and Steel.* Pittsburgh: University of Pittsburgh Press, 1992.

Kunhardt, Philip B., Jr., et al. *P. T. Barnum: America's Greatest Showman.* New York: Knopf, 1995.

McKinley, E. H. *Marching to Glory: The History of the Salvation Army in the United States, 1880–1992.* Grand Rapids, Mich.: William B. Eerdmans Publishing Co., 1995.

The Daniel A. P. Murray Collection, 1818–1907. The National Archives.

Peskin, Allan. *Garfield: A Biography.* Kent, Ohio: Kent State University Press, 1978.

Robinson, Charles M., III. *The Men Who Wore the Star: The Story of the Texas Rangers.* New York: Random House, 2000.

Zimmer, William F. *Frontier Soldier: An Enlisted Man's Journal of the Sioux and Nez Perce Campaign, 1877.* Edited and annotated by Jerome A. Greene. Helena, Mont.: The Montana Historical Society Press, 1998.

Online Sources

Online sources are an excellent way to obtain primary source historical documents and related material. Especially helpful are the five Web sites listed in part A, which are not listed in alphabetical order but instead by their degree of value to the historian. Descriptions of these sites are provided. Part B lists other Web sites that may prove helpful in the search for primary source historical information.

Part A.

The National Archives
http://www.nara.gov

Provides a wide variety of pages, including lessons on primary sources. An excellent place to start a search for historical documents or information on the Web.

The Library of Congress
http://www.loc.gov

Offers extensive holdings of historical documents and information, including the American Memory collection.

The Presidential Library System
http://www.nara.gov/exhall/treasures/preslib.html

Provides access to the Presidential Library System through the National Archives. Visitors may review papers and holdings of presidents from Hoover to Clinton.

Yale University
http://www.library.yale.edu

Lists over one thousand Web sites and holdings, including more than one hundred entries under Primary Sources American History. Connects to Archives USA and The National Union Catalog of Manuscript Collections, The National Inventory of Documentary Sources, and The Directory of Archives and Manuscript Repositories in the U.S.

University of Michigan Documents Center
http://www.lib.umich.edu/libhome/Documents.center/index.html

Contains large holding of U.S. government publications.

Part B.

Historical Speeches Archive
www.webcorp.com/sounds/index.html

Historical Text Archive
http://www.historicaltextarchive.com

The News Film Library
http://www.sc.edu/newsfilm/film.htm

The Ohio Historical Society
http://www.ohiohistory.org/resource/teachers/primary.html

U.S. and State Flags
http://www.law.ou.edu/fedflag.html

U.S. Historical Documents
http://history.cc.ukans.edu/carrie/docs/texts/usdocs.html

U.S. Historical Documents
http://www.law.ou.edu/hist

U.S. Historical Documents
http://www.moa.umdl.umich.edu

Acknowledgments

For permission to reprint all works in this volume, grateful acknowledgment is made to the following holders of copyright, publishers, or representatives.

Lesson 2, Handout 5

For use of the photograph of a ticket wagon, Barnum & Bailey, 1888. Circus World Museum, Baraboo, Wisconsin. Used with permission.

For use of the photograph of a horse-drawn tableau wagon. From the collection of Howard Tibbals. Used by permission.

For use of the photograph of Negative #16,382. Barnum elephants, Old Home Week. Town House Square. Courtesy Peabody Essex Museum.

For use of the photograph of a side show talker and snake charmer, Barnum & Bailey, 1888. Circus World Museum, Baraboo, Wisconsin. Used with permission.

Lesson 2, Handout 6

For use of advertisement for the Barnum and Bailey circus. Reprinted by permission of the Bridgeport, Conn., Public Library.

Lesson 3, Handout 7

For use of an excerpt from *Frontier Soldier: An Enlisted Man's Journal of the Sioux and Nez Perce Campaign, 1877*, Jerome A. Greene, editor, William F. Zimmer (Montana Historical Society Press, Helena, 1998). Used with permission.

Lesson 3, Handout 8

For use of illustrations by Red Horse, National Anthropological Archives, Smithsonian Institution. Used with permission.

Lesson 4, Handout 9

For use of cover of the dime novel *The Bradys and the Chinese Dwarf.* Courtesy of the Department of Special Collections, Stanford University Libraries.

Lesson 10, Handout 25

For use of the advertisement for the Arcade Restaurant and Chop House. Courtesy of the Arizona Historical Society/Tucson. AHS #79325.

For use of the program for "The Hunchback," August 1875. California Historical Society, Theatre Ephemera Collection, North Baker Research Library. Used with permission.

For use of the advertisement for Frances C. Treadwell, Lady Dentist from "San Francisco Business Directory," S.F.: San Francisco Directory Company, 1892–94. California Historical Society, North Baker Research Library; FN-23068. Used with permission.

For use of Wells Fargo Agent's Certificate, Cassie Hill, 1884. In the collection of Wells Fargo Bank. Used with permission.

For use of teaching certificate, Belle M. Crose, 1883. In the collection of the Nebraska State Historical Society. Used with permission.

For use of homestead deed, Josephine Howard, 1889. In the collection of the Nebraska State Historical Society. Used with permission.

Social Studies Series

Advanced Placement
Advanced Placement U.S. History, Book 1 (Teacher and Student Editions)
Advanced Placement U.S. History, Book 2 (Teacher and Student Editions)
Advanced Placement Economics
Advanced Placement European History, Book 1 (Teacher and Student Editions)
Advanced Placement European History, Book 2 (Teacher and Student Editions)
Advanced Placement U.S. Government and Politics (Teacher and Student Editions)

Basic Skills
Basic Skills: Geography
Basic Skills: Government
Basic Skills: United States History
Basic Skills: World Cultures/World History

Economics
Economics, Book 1: Microeconomics and the American Economy
Economics, Book 2: Macroeconomics and the American Economy
Fundamentals of Economics: Making Your Way in Our Economy (Teacher Manual and Student Workbook)

Government
U.S. Government, Book 1: We, the People
U.S. Government, Book 2: Government of the People and by the People

Issues
American Social Issues
Contemporary Issues
Current Issues in Global Education
Issues in Our Changing World

Cross-Curriculum
Peer Mediation: Training Students in Conflict Resolution
The Positive Teacher: Daily Reflections
Searching for Yourself
Supervisor/Student Teacher Manual
Valuing Others

Primary Sources in U.S. History
Colonization: 1521–1763
Revolution and Constitution: 1763–1791
Early Nation: 1791–1820*
Jacksonian America: 1820–1840
Antebellum America and Civil War: 1840–1865
Reconstruction: 1865–1877
Expansive America: 1877–1898
America in the Age of Imperialism: 1898–1920*
Interwar America: 1920–1940
America in World War II: The 1940s
Consensus and Conformity: The 1950s
America in Upheaval: The 1960s
Disillusioned America: The 1970s
America's Turn to the Right: The 1980s*
Technological Revolution: The 1990s*

Senior High Electives
Anthropology
Philosophy
Psychology
Sociology

Social Issues
American Education: Exploring School Reform
The American Family
America's Children
Censorship
The Deficit and National Debt
The Environment
Issues in the Workplace
Juvenile Justice: In the Hands of the Law
Teens and Alcohol

United States History
U.S. History, Book 1: Beginning–1865
U.S. History, Book 2: 1866–1920
U.S. History, Book 3: 1920–1960
U.S. History, Book 4: 1960–1990

World History
World History, Book 1: Beginning–1200 A.D.
World History, Book 2: 1201–1814
World History, Book 3: 1815–1919
World History, Book 4: 1920–1992

** To be published*

The Center for Learning

The Publisher

All instructional materials identified by the TAP® (Teachers/Authors/Publishers) trademark are developed by a national network of teachers whose collective educational experience distinguishes the publishing objective of The Center for Learning, a nonprofit educational corporation founded in 1970.

Concentrating on values-related disciplines, the Center publishes humanities and religion curriculum units for use in public and private schools and other educational settings. Approximately 500 language arts, social studies, novel/drama, life issues, and faith publications are available.

While acutely aware of the challenges and uncertain solutions to growing educational problems, the Center is committed to quality curriculum development and to the expansion of learning opportunities for all students. Publications are regularly evaluated and updated to meet the changing and diverse needs of teachers and students. Teachers may offer suggestions for development of new publications or revisions of existing titles by contacting

The Center for Learning

Administrative/Editorial Office
21590 Center Ridge Rd.
Rocky River, OH 44116
(440) 331-1404 • FAX (440) 331-5414
E-mail: cfl@stratos.net
Web: http://www.centerforlearning.org

For a free catalog containing order and price information and a descriptive listing of titles, contact

The Center for Learning

Shipping/Business Office
P.O. Box 910
Villa Maria, PA 16155
(724) 964-8083 • (800) 767-9090
FAX (888) 767-8080